Balboa Park
A MILLENNIUM HISTORY
by Roger M. Showley

Text Copyright ©1999: Roger M. Showley

Photo Editor: Gregory L. Williams

Contributing Photographer: Robert A. Eplett

Publisher: C.E. Parks

Editor-in-Chief: Lori M. Parks

VP/National Sales Manager: Ray Spagnuolo

VP/Corporate Development: Bart Barica

CFO: Randall Peterson

Managing Editor: Betsy Baxter Blondin

Production Manager: Deborah Sherwood

Art Director: Gina Mancini

Graphic Designer: Jeff Caton

Production Staff: Jason Atzert, Sean Gates,
Brad Hartman, Dave Hermstead,
Jay Kennedy, John Leyva, Barry Miller, Susie Passons, Norm Pruitt,
Chris Rivera, Steve Trainor

Coordinating Editors: Renee Kim, Betsy Lelja,
Elizabeth Lex, Sara Rufner, Adriane Wessels, John Woodward

Administration Manager: Ellen Ruby

Administration: Juan Diaz, Emily Knopp, Majka Penner, Scott Reid,
Patrick Rucker, Cory Sottek

Published by

Heritage Media Corp.

6354 Corte del Abeto, Suite B

Carlsbad, California 92009

www.heritagemedia.com

Printed by Heritage Media Corp. in the United States of America

San Diego Historical Society

For Carol

Table of Contents

Foreword

Call the roll of great visionaries in San Diego's history and you'll find most played an essential part in making Balboa Park what it is today: Ephraim Morse, George Marston, Samuel Parsons, Charles Collier, Kate Sessions, Bertram Goodhue, John Spreckels, Dr. Harry Wegeforth, Gertrude Gilbert, Frank Drugan, Richard Requa, Bea Evenson... If some of these aren't known to you, you'll learn in Roger Showley's book who they were and what roles they played in making Balboa Park the centerpiece that it is in our city's geography and in its tourism promotions.

It's not, of course, suggested these were the only key people involved in Balboa Park's evolution; there have been countless others who've contributed — and others who still are — with their visions, their advocacy and their works. It's safe to say "works" in the plural because of the legions of people, most of them unnamed, who have labored, now work, or will in the future, at the park's institutions, as well as for the City of San Diego. The latter is much involved in the story, for as you'll learn in this book, the city owns all of the park's land, gardens, structures and even the zoo's animals.

My love for Balboa Park began at an early age, I think — in utero, for I was born in 1915, and surely my mother visited the park in that auspicious year. My proximity grew when, from 1927 to 1933, I attended Roosevelt Junior High and then San Diego High School, both within the park's original 1,400 acres. I had to cross those acres, usually by bicycle, five days a week to get to school. What Roger doesn't tell is that the girl who later became my wife of 42 years worked as a cashier at the 1935-36 expo, and some nights it was a challenge to learn where she was assigned so that I could pick her up at the end of her shift.

I think the most stirring part of Balboa Park's story is that of the 1915 exposition, which commenced in 1909 when G. Aubrey Davidson, an immigrant from Canada, envisioned a world's fair to celebrate completion of the Panama Canal, which was then being built. He sold his idea to the San Diego Chamber of Commerce and in 1911 a four-day groundbreaking festival was held and attended by great crowds. Then, promoters like Charlie Collier, financiers like Joe Sefton Jr. and Julius Wangenheim, investors like John D. Spreckels, architects like Bertram Goodhue, builders like Frank P. Allen and their associates went to work.

On the night of December 31, 1914, at opening ceremonies attended by thousands, the Panama-California Exposition was dedicated with all the construction finished on time and under budget. Perhaps the most incredible of all, these acres of buildings and gardens, which for their beauty and charm would bring international fame to San Diego and a lasting center of culture for our townsfolk and tourists, had been created by a city whose population was only 50,000!

Now, at the Second Millennium's end, sometimes more than 50,000 will visit Balboa Park on a single day. And that popularity reminds us of some of the park's problems. Despite the free trolleys that can take people from parking lots to and from where they want to go, parking and traffic congestion on too many days can be challenges.

As one learns from Roger's pages, an approved master plan and subordinate precise plans for Balboa Park exist. But they need to be adhered to and updated from time to time — by people who, like their forebears, have vision.

Philip M. Klauber
August 1999

ZURBARAN

Introduction & **Acknowledgments**

What is your favorite historic site? Is it Colonial Williamsburg in Virginia or the Acropolis in Greece, a Buddhist shrine in Japan or the pyramids of Egypt? For me, it's Balboa Park. By world standards, it's not a really ancient place. Its history is rather thin and contrived, a manmade landscape of mostly imported plants and architecture never intended to last this long.

But San Diegans and visitors from around the world marvel at the place. Sometimes, I'll pause in the Alcazar Garden as I rush to a play at the Old Globe. I look up at the majestic California Tower and silently thank past generations for creating, preserving and maintaining what I think is the world's greatest urban park. Balboa Park has it all — culture, nature, playgrounds, gardens — and the San Diego Zoo.

And yet, Balboa Park has its limits. Some doubters in the early years, as you will learn, said San Diego would never need such a large expanse of open space. Let's sell half or more to developers, they said, and use the proceeds to balance the budget or build neighborhood parks around the city. Nearly 300 acres have been lost to nonpark uses, including schools, freeways and the Naval Hospital. Hundreds more acres are occupied by museums and the zoo — cultural riches that once were free to visit but now, because of limited taxpayer support, charge ever-rising admissions. Dozens of recreational, social and performing arts groups occupy buildings scattered about the park. They offer members and the general public many worthwhile programs. But almost no one speaks for the park, just pieces of it. And that's part of the motivation for writing this book. With greater knowledge of the park's history and appreciation for its treasures, more San Diegans, I hope, will defend the park as a whole, fight for its improvement and fend off incursions.

In the bibliography are additional sources you may wish to consult if you would like to delve further. Two bear repeating here. First is the late Florence Christman's *Romance of Balboa Park*. First published by the San Diego Historical Society in 1969, it has been periodically updated and remains the most readily available source for information about the exposition buildings. Second is historian Richard Amero's vast collection of news articles and documents, carefully copied and stored in dozens of three-ring binders at the San Diego Historical Society's research archives in the park. He spent more than 20 years gathering this material for research articles he submitted to the society's *Journal of San Diego History* and other publications. I spent three months of weekends going through the entire collection, gathering what I needed for this book. Without his labors, it would have taken me years. Mr. Amero graciously agreed to read the manuscript and offered many suggested changes that have been incorporated. For both his collection and his advice, I am very grateful.

Other park lovers helped me untangle the park's history and my sometimes garbled syntax. They included Philip M. Klauber, Welton Jones, Peggy and Hamilton Marston, Betty and Homer Peabody, Kim Duclo, Peggy Lacy, Steve Estrada, Penny Scott, Pat DeMarce, Judy Swink and Laura Walcher. Bob Witty, Greg Williams and John Panter, newly added to the San Diego Historical Society staff, helped get the project going and, at lightning speed, gathered up the best photographs and graphic material to illustrate the text. I thank them all. Also helpful were assistant archivist Dennis Sharp and former archivists Rick Crawford and Sally West, whose exhibition on Samuel Parsons Jr. and other park master plans convinced me that a new book on the park's history was needed. One other thank you goes to Mary Ward, county historian, who before her death in January 1999 suggested the cover artwork for this book, a 1916 painting by Charles A. Fries that she owned.

No doubt, some mistakes have slipped through. If you notice any, please let me know so they can be corrected in later editions. I also thank the zoo, museums, organizations and institutions for providing information about their origins. My greatest hope would be that this book will inspire them to compile their own histories so that future generations may learn more about the people who made and maintain the park.

My gratitude also goes to Heritage Media Corporation, for which this work was something of a departure from its usual run of history books. I hope it proves to be a profitable gamble, because virtually every great city has a great park, with a history waiting to be told in such a first-class way. Even New York's Central Park lacks a splendidly illustrated history of this kind. What would be more appropriate than for the company's owners, Charles and Lori Parks, to commission a series of histories of the nation's — even the world's — great urban parks!

Finally, I want to thank my wife, Carol, to whom this book is dedicated. Many nights, after we put our children, Charlie and Cookie, to bed, she didn't see me until after midnight, as I pounded away on my iMac to get the manuscript in shape. As an architecture student in Spain, Carol learned to appreciate Hispanic art and architecture and, as a relative newcomer to San Diego, she's come to love Balboa Park as much as I. She takes the kids to the zoo, rides with them on the carousel and miniature railroad and meets me for weekday picnics in the Pepper Grove. Parks are for lovers and we both love to be in Balboa Park.

Roger M. Showley
August 1999

ZURBARAN

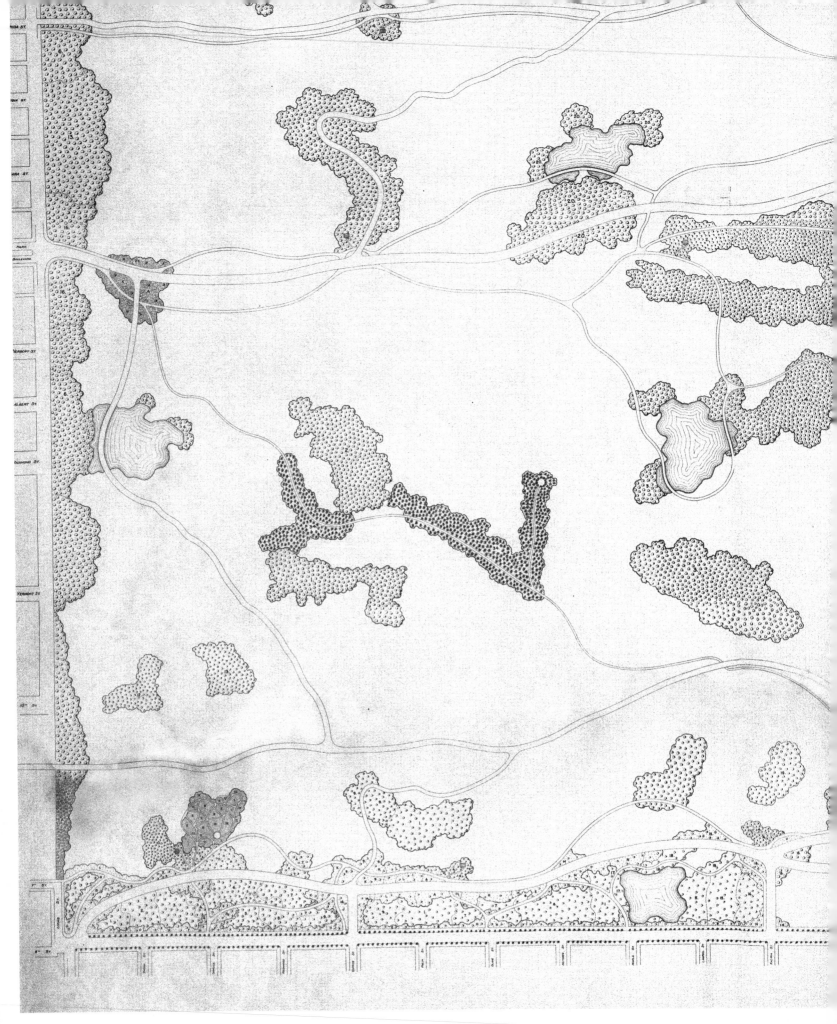

THE FIRST MASTER PLAN FOR BALBOA PARK BY SAMUEL PARSONS JR., 1905 *San Diego Historical Society*

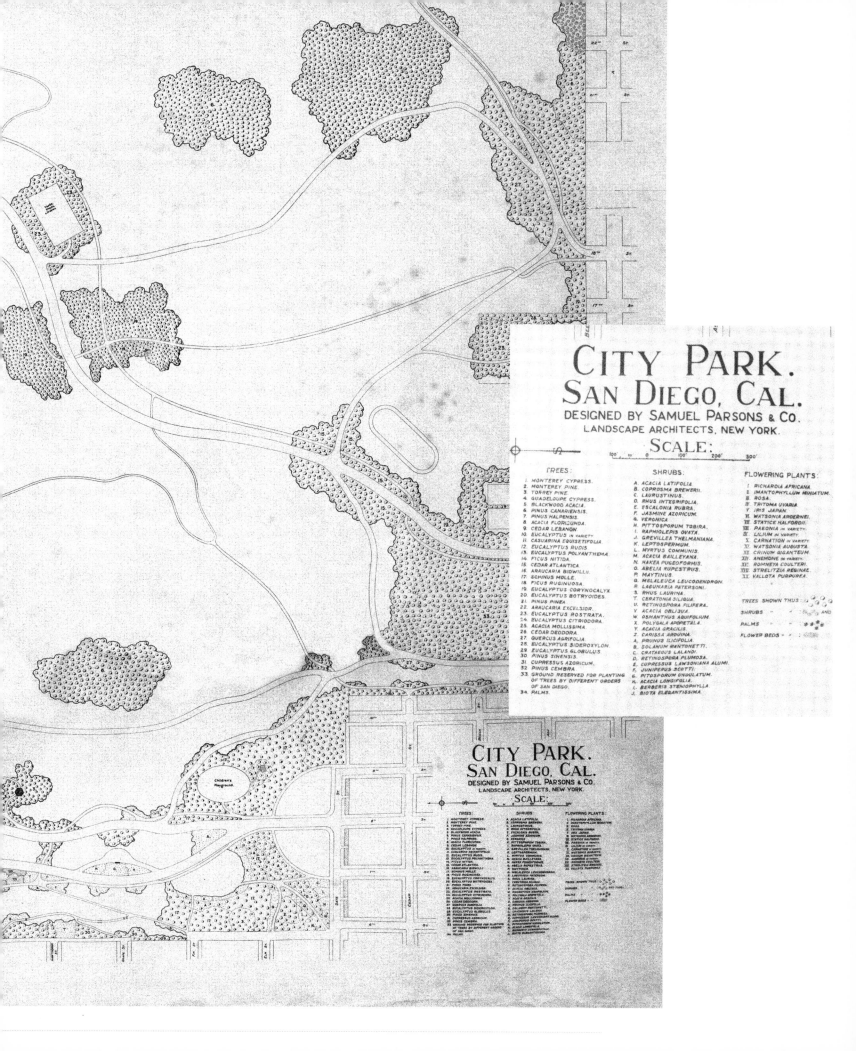

CITY PARK.
SAN DIEGO, CAL.
DESIGNED BY SAMUEL PARSONS & CO.
LANDSCAPE ARCHITECTS, NEW YORK.
SCALE:

100'   50   0   100'   200'   300'

TREES:	SHRUBS:	FLOWERING PLANTS:
1. MONTEREY CYPRESS.	A. ACACIA LATIFOLIA.	I. RICHARDIA AFRICANA.
2. MONTEREY PINE.	B. COPROSMA BREWERII.	II. IMANTOPHYLLUM MINIATUM.
3. TORREY PINE.	C. LAURUSTINUS.	III. ROSA.
4. GUADELOUPE CYPRESS.	D. RHUS INTEGRIFOLIA.	IV. TRITOMA UVARIA.
5. BLACKWOOD ACACIA.	E. ESCALONIA RUBRA.	V. IRIS JAPAN.
6. PINUS CANARIENSIS.	F. JASMINE AZORICUM.	VI. WATSONIA ARDERNEI.
7. PINUS HALPENSIS.	G. VERONICA.	VII. STATICE HALFORDII.
8. ACACIA FLORIBUNDA.	H. PITTOSPORUM TOBIRA.	VIII. PAEONIA IN VARIETY.
9. CEDAR LEBANON.	I. RAPHIOLEPIS OVATA.	IX. LILIUM IN VARIETY.
10. EUCALYPTUS IN VARIETY.	J. GREVILLEA THELMANIANA.	X. CARNATION IN VARIETY.
11. CASUARINA EQUISETIFOLIA.	K. LEPTOSPERMUM.	XI. WATSONIA AUGUSTA.
12. EUCALYPTUS RUDIS.	L. MYRTUS COMMUNIS.	XII. CRINUM GIGANTEUM.
13. EUCALYPTUS POLYANTHEMA.	M. ACACIA BAILLEYANA.	XIII. ANEMONE IN VARIETY.
14. FICUS NITIDA.	N. HAKEA PUGEOFORMIS.	XIV. ROMNEYA COULTERI.
15. CEDAR ATLANTICA.	O. ABELIA RUPESTRUS.	XV. STRELITZIA REGINAE.
16. ARAUCARIA BIDWILLII.	P. MAYTINUS.	XVI. VALLOTA PURPUREA.
17. SCHINUS MOLLE.	Q. MELALEUCA LEUCODENDRON.	
18. FICUS RUGINUOSA.	R. LAGUNARIA PATERSONI.	
19. EUCALYPTUS CORYNOCALYX.	S. RHUS LAURINA.	
20. EUCALYPTUS BOTRYOIDES.	T. CERATONIA SILIQUA.	
21. PINUS PINEA.	U. RETINOSPORA FILIFERA.	TREES SHOWN THUS:
22. ARAUCARIA EXCELSIOR.	V. ACACIA OBLIQUA.	
23. EUCALYPTUS ROSTRATA.	W. OSMANTHUS AQUIFOLIUM.	SHRUBS — AND
24. EUCALYPTUS CITRIODORA.	X. POLYGALA APPETALA.	
25. ACACIA MOLLISSIMA.	Y. ACACIA GRACILIS.	PALMS —
26. CEDAR DEODORA.	Z. CARISSA ARDUINA.	
27. QUERCUS AGRIFOLIA.	A. PRUNUS ILICIFOLIA.	FLOWER BEDS —
28. EUCALYPTUS SIDEROXYLON.	B. SOLANUM RANTONETTI.	
29. EUCALYPTUS GLOBULUS.	C. CRATAEGUS LALANDI.	
30. PINUS SINENSIS.	D. RETINOSPORA PLUMOSA.	
31. CUPRESSUS AZORICUM.	E. CUPRESSUS LAWSONIANA ALUMI.	
32. PINUS CEMBRA.	F. JUNIPERUS SCOTTI.	
33. GROUND RESERVED FOR PLANTING OF TREES BY DIFFERENT ORDERS OF SAN DIEGO.	G. PITOSPORUM UNDULATUM.	
	H. ACACIA LONGIFOLIA.	
34. PALMS.	I. BERBERIS STENIOPHYLLA.	
	J. BIOTA ELEGANTISSIMA.	

Children's Playground.

CITY PARK.
SAN DIEGO, CAL.
DESIGNED BY SAMUEL PARSONS & CO.
LANDSCAPE ARCHITECTS, NEW YORK.
SCALE:

TREES: SHRUBS: FLOWERING PLANTS:

A Grand
OPPORTUNITY
1868 — 1909

Robert A. Epler

Chapter One

"*Every park has its own peculiar and more or less distinct characteristics, but this great area of spreading mesas and rugged, picturesque canyons is markedly different from all other parks I have seen in Europe and America... There is nothing like it among the parks of the world.*"

— *Samuel Parsons Jr., 1902*

alboa Park came into being on a whim. A perfectly situated oasis of cultural treasures in an urban garden, it was not always so beautiful and beloved. It languished in an undeveloped state for decades and nearly disappeared in the course of repeated attempts to sell it, parcel it out and pave it over.

Unlike New York which bought $5 million worth of land in the 1850s on which to build Central Park, San Diego got what at first was called "City Park" for free. It was part of the original 48,500 acres of public lands San Diego received when the Mexican government granted it pueblo status in 1835. New York had to clear its 800-acre park of farmlands and squatter housing. San Diego's park was a largely uninhabited, treeless expanse of mesas and canyons covered by low chaparral and wildflowers.

But park planning and development were not on the new city's agenda. Only about 500 people lived in Old Town at the time and growth was slow, even after the United States seized California during the Mexican-American War of 1846-48. The only "park" was Old Town's central plaza, renamed Washington Square after the American conquest.

Horton spurs change

Alonzo E. Horton changed that. A San Francisco furniture dealer, Horton visited in San Diego in April 1867 after hearing of its potential and, encouraged by town trustee Ephraim W. Morse, bought 800 acres of present-day downtown at public auction for $265 and proceeded to move the city center near to the waterfront.

Toward the end of his term, Morse apparently believed that other investors would approach the city to buy more land and he won agreement from the other two trustees, J.S. Manasse and Thomas Bush, to set aside two pueblo lots of 160 acres each "for the purpose of securing to the inhabitants of the city of San Diego a suitable park." Morse was a determined backyard gardener and, having spent his youth in Amesbury, Massachusetts, knew well the pleasures of that city's Common. He also was familiar with the development of New York's Central Park.

Horton joined Morse in choosing the park site for obvious reasons. Placing the park adjacent to his property would presumably increase its value. The two friends walked the rough terrain and decided to recommend a much larger park — nine pueblo lots

SAN DIEGO, CORONADO, NORTH ISLAND AND POINT LOMA — UNDEVELOPED BALBOA PARK IS IN THE LOWER PART OF THE LITHOGRAPH, 1876.

San Diego Historical Society

OLD TOWN. MISSION BAY AND POINT LOMA IN BACKGROUND, 1898 *San Diego Historical Society*

ALONZO E. HORTON
(1813-1909)
PURCHASED PRESENT DAY
DOWNTOWN SAN DIEGO
FOR $265 IN 1867. HE ALSO
ASSISTED IN THE SELECTION
OF THE SITE OF THE PARK.
San Diego Historical Society

EPHRAIM W. MORSE
(1823-1906),
SAN DIEGO PIONEER. AS A
TOWN TRUSTEE HE
INTRODUCED A RESOLUTION
TO RESERVE LAND FOR THE
FUTURE BALBOA PARK.
San Diego Historical Society

JAMES MCCOY
(1821-1895)
WAS A CALIFORNIA STATE
SENATOR FROM SAN DIEGO,
WHO AFTER SERVING AS A
CITY TRUSTEE, ATTEMPTED TO
UNDO THE RESERVATION OF
1,400 ACRES FOR CITY PARK.
San Diego Historical Society

totaling 1,400 acres for the park, north and east of Horton's Addition. What a convenient buffer — and amenity — around Horton's properties! Rivals were none too few: Trustee Manasse's lumberyard manager Matthew Carruthers and his wife Isabella had bought 40 acres of the southwest corner of one of the park pueblo lots for $175 on February 13, 1868, just two days before Morse introduced his motion to identify and reserve the parkland. This property is now referred to as Cortez Hill and includes the historic El Cortez Hotel.

On May 26, 1868, Morse was ready with his site proposal. A new set of trustees had taken office — José Guadalupe Estudillo, Marcus Schiller and Joshua Sloane — and they unanimously approved this resolution for a park reservation:

"Moved and seconded that Lots 1131, 1130, 1129, 1135, 1136, 1137, vacant part of 1144, 1143, 1142 be for a park."

Decades later, Estudillo and Sloane took credit for pushing for the park. At the 1915 Panama-California Exposition, the 47th anniversary of the City Park resolution was declared Estudillo Day. Estudillo, the last surviving park founder, declared: "I suggested that 1,400 acres be set aside as a public park. I really didn't have in mind that the land should be used for a park, but merely

as a means of saving it for the city… And that is the story of the origin of the park."

Sloane, an Irish immigrant who served as postmaster and Board of Trustees clerk, continued his defense of the park. In later years, one of his friends asserted, "He was the man who first proposed a big park here and he urged it on the trustees till they let him have his way; he stood like a bulldog over that park, and someday people will be grateful to him for doing so. His mission here seemed to be, 'Save that Park,' and he did it." All three trustees received due recognition in 1928, when a bronze plaque was placed in their honor at the entrance to El Prado.

Park dismantlers and defenders

The park needed stout, tireless defenders, for threats soon surfaced to reduce it in size or sell it off for development. In those days, all trustee actions required ratification by the Legislature in Sacramento. By October 1869, yet another set of trustees was in charge — Estudillo, who had been reelected, James McCoy, a former sheriff, and Matthew Sherman, a Civil War veteran (and subdivider of Sherman Heights, east of Horton's property). They requested legislative approval of the park reservation. When a group of San Diegans attempted to remove 480 acres from the east side of the

DANIEL CLEVELAND
(1838-1929),
FORMER MAYOR OF SAN
ANTONIO WHO SET UP A
LAW PRACTICE IN SAN
DIEGO AND DEFENDED CITY
PARK FROM ITS DETRACTORS.
HE HELPED FOUND THE
SOCIETY OF NATURAL
HISTORY IN 1874 AND THE
SAN DIEGO ART
ASSOCIATION IN 1904.
San Diego Historical Society

NEWLY CONSTRUCTED BUILDINGS AND VICTORIAN HOUSES AT THE CORNER OF SIXTH AVENUE AND E STREET WITH UNDEVELOPED CITY PARK IN DISTANCE, c. 1887
San Diego Historical Society

park and acquire them for private development, former trustee Sloane gathered 160 signatures on a petition to support the full 1,400-acre park.

"If San Diego is to become an important city, as seems now generally conceded to be her destiny, we, like other cities, must have our public park," *The San Diego Union* editorialized. "Let us take an interest in this matter and assist in preserving for ourselves and our children this park reservation. Let us by our private sympathy, conversation and influence and by our public action resist to the bitter end all bad men who seek to take this away from us. With this park, we have a perpetual source of pride and satisfaction; without it, of shame, and bitter unavailing regrets." The Legislature made no changes and on February 4, 1870, approved "An Act To Insure the Permanence of the Reservation," declaring "These lands ... are to be held in trust forever by the municipal authorities of said city for the use and purposes of a public park and for no other or different purpose."

However, the Legislature's act did not stand uncontested. By late-1871, city Trustee McCoy had been elected state senator over Alonzo Horton. Even though he had supported the park locally,

McCoy took advantage of his new position to undo the park reservation. Tipped off by a San Diegan who happened to be in Sacramento at the time, city Trustee Sherman joined with Daniel Cleveland, a former mayor of San Antonio, Texas, and a dozen others to collect signatures from virtually every registered voter to oppose the bill by McCoy and San Diego Assemblyman George M. Dannals. Among the petition signers: a 21-year-old newcomer named George W. Marston, destined to become the city's number one merchant, benefactor and park defender.

Cleveland, writing about the incident 55 years later, vividly recalled the firestorm that swept San Diego:

"Within a few hours, the whole city was thoroughly canvassed and every man [women did not yet have the vote] who could be reached had signed the petition. There were 366 signatures in all. All the papers were then gathered in and the petition was again printed with the names...

"Within about four days from the time the news of the introduction of this iniquitous bill reached San Diego, a copy of this petition with all the signatures was in the hands of every member of the Legislature. This petition killed the McCoy bill, and up to this time [1926], and finally , we hope, has put an end to all legislative action prejudicial to Balboa Park."

Pound, pest house and gunpowder

Over the next 15 years, the 1,400-acre open space — known as "City Park" — lay unimproved and became something of a dumping ground for activities incompatible with life down by the bay. An animal pound was established in the westernmost canyon, where stray horses and cattle were herded until they could be claimed. The San Diego Water Company drilled a well in the canyon and built two reservoirs on the mesa overlooking the canyon. Arnold Wentscher, the city's first German consul, and, John G. Capron, a merchant, built gunpowder houses in two other canyons. Near 28th Street just east of the eastern park boundary, was a "pest house" where people with smallpox and other communicable diseases were quarantined.

Meanwhile, at Eighth Avenue and Date Street, an Indian *ranchería* or small hamlet continued undisturbed. Residents sometimes complained of their presence. "The Indians frightened my mother terribly sometimes," recalled Harriet Goodbody, whose father, E.D. Switzer, farmed five acres on the edge of what came to be called Switzer Canyon. "One day she was using her sewing machine and looking up she saw staring in through the window a great big black savage.

The Indians were always very curious about what we did and would watch everything. They used to cause quite a good deal of trouble by taking what did not belong to them."

As early as 1873, City Park was seen as an ideal spot for public schools. "The southwestern corner of this reservation contains the finest location for public school buildings that can be found in the city," the *Union* said. "Here there is a gently sloping eminence which commands a view of the whole city, the bay and the ocean beyond... Why should not, say 10 acres, be taken in this portion of the park for the public school buildings and grounds? A most desirable site can here be obtained without cost — a site which possesses the advantages of healthfulness, a magnificent view, nearness to the center of population, yet sufficiently removed from the noise and bustle of the city and from the danger of fire."

And so it was not surprising that on August 8, 1881, when the city needed a new school site, the Board of Trustees approved the use of five acres for construction of what became San Diego High School. (The original school opened in 1882; a lease was not signed until 1974, expiring in 2024.)

Boom time

The 1880s witnessed an extraordinary boom in San Diego with the arrival of train service. The city's population soared from about 5,000 to 40,000 by 1887 before the inevitable bust. But left behind were many stately Victorian offices, hotels and commercial establishments that comprise today's Gaslamp Quarter along Fifth Avenue downtown.

The economic upswing prompted George Marston, Abraham Klauber and other businessmen in December 1884 to seek approval to plant eucalyptus trees and make other improvements at their own expense in City Park. The

FIFTH AVENUE NEAR G STREET, DOWNTOWN SAN DIEGO, DURING ECONOMIC BOOM C. 1888 *San Diego Historical Society*

HOTEL DEL CORONADO UNDER CONSTRUCTION, 1887 *San Diego Historical Society*

group conducted a field survey in January but did not carry out their plans. In 1886, Elisha Babcock and H.L. Story, who were developing the Hotel del Coronado and the rest of Coronado at this time, built a steam-powered streetcar line, the University Heights Motor Road (known popularly as the Park Belt Line) up Switzer Canyon toward what is today North Park. Businessman Levi Chase advocated selling half the park to reduce it to a manageable size of only 640 acres. The U.S. Army requested a park site in exchange for its barracks site downtown. Even Marston endorsed the barracks land swap.

"In my limited acquaintance," one letter writer identified as "Progress" wrote the *Union*, "I find that there are a good many people who think that the reservation of more than 1,400 acres of land forever for park purposes is an absurd piece of folly; some

are of the opinion that a park of 600 acres is a pretty big thing to take care of. Why should the handsomest residences in the city be forever locked up?"

But park defenders shot back with warnings against short-sightedness. The Citizens Association for Improving and Beautifying San Diego, headed by Bryant Howard, submitted a petition in December 1886 signed by 250 residents opposed to dividing up the park: "We are opposed to the sale of even one foot of it," said John G. Capron, the gunpowder house advocate of a decade earlier. "If we once began to meddle with the park, we might as well say good-bye to the whole thing." A group of property owners also opposed the land sale, apparently worried about competition from city-owned lots for sale. The trustees adjourned the meeting for the New Year's holidays and nothing more came of the idea.

Howard's charity tract approved

In 1887, park ideas continued to be advanced, including a proposal by Chamber of Commerce President G.G. Brandt to locate a permanent county fairgrounds, observatory, custom house and other public buildings there. "Surely we have more land in that park than will be needed for park purposes for the next half-century, if indeed it is ever to be made useful for such purposes," Brandt wrote the *Union*. "Then why not make use of it for our more immediate wants? Now, Mr. Editor, lend your journal as a powerful influence towards having something done to our present worthless park."

The Board of Trustees finally gave in to the plea to make something of the park land. The request came from the self-same Bryant Howard and Ephraim Morse, who had opposed earlier development proposals. In November 1887, they requested 100 acres on Inspiration Point (future home of the Balboa Naval Hospital), on which to build an orphanage, a free kindergarten, a boys and girls aid society home and an industrial and technology school. They had an astounding $600,000 in pledges and bequests and promised to return the land to the city if the endeavor failed.

"While we can, without cost, obtain the land necessary for our purpose and a large bonus also by locating these institutions elsewhere," Howard told the trustees, "we are desirous of placing them within easy access of the larger number of those they are intended to benefit, and besides, we wish to avoid the appearance of and even the suspicion of being engaged in a speculation."

On December 2, 1887, the trustees approved the plan along with a five-acre grant to the Women's Home Association for a haven for indigent women. George Marston spoke out against the Howard Tract as setting a dangerous precedent. He wrote, perhaps for the first time, that what was needed was a "comprehensive plan" and control of the park "entirely under one board of commissioners." San Diego may be small, he wrote the *Union*, but it will need a large park "of grand proportions and capabilities" as it grows. The editors replied that the city of the future would need many parks, not just one big one "behind one fence... No, let us have some of the city park opened to the hand of private improvement and charity, and we answer for it that the millions of San Diegans who will be here in 1989 won't bewail the forethought which prompted the concession."

The property was landscaped and two buildings opened October 7, 1890, serving 15 kindergartners the first year. But Howard was unable to secure title to the property and the school closed down after the second year. The 1893 national financial panic wiped out the charities' funds and in 1896 the property reverted to the city. A caretaker occupied the three-story home until fire destroyed it May 11, 1897, one month after the city insured it for $4,000. Meanwhile the Women's Home Association opened a 10-room indigent women's residential facility and day nursery, which remained on park property until freeway construction forced its relocation in the 1950s.

CHILDREN'S INDUSTRIAL INSTITUTE IN THE PARK WAS CONSTRUCTED IN 1889 AND DESTROYED BY FIRE IN 1897, C. 1892. *San Diego Historical Society*

KATE O. SESSIONS
(1857-1940),
SAN DIEGO'S LEADING
HORTICULTURIST, LEASED
32 ACRES IN THE NORTH-
WEST CORNER OF CITY
PARK IN 1892 IN WHICH TO
OPERATE HER NURSERY. SHE
INTRODUCED MANY EXOTIC
PLANTS INTO THE PARK AND
AROUND THE CITY. A STATUE
IN HER HONOR WAS
INSTALLED ON LAUREL
STREET NEAR SIXTH
AVENUE IN 1998.
San Diego Historical Society

CHILDREN'S HOME AT 16TH AND ASH, HOSPITAL AT LEFT, BOY'S DORM IN CENTER AND OLD STRUCTURE AT RIGHT, 1909
San Diego Historical Society

San Diego women take charge

The Howard Tract experience may have prompted pro-park San Diegans to action. In 1889, the Ladies Annex of the San Diego Chamber of Commerce took the first step toward systematically landscaping the park. Marking the first of many actions by San Diego women to secure, develop and maintain the park, the wives of chamber members raised more than $500 to plant 13.9 acres between Juniper and Palm streets. They were led by Emma Lake, whose husband Ben ran the Stanford House on F Street, and they took their task seriously. The women drew on their knowledge of picturesque landscaping principles then in vogue and San Diego's leading horticulturist, Kate O. Sessions, advised where to plant about 700 trees and shrubs.

"We thoroughly appreciate the necessity of beautifying a portion of our City Park," the women said in a report, "for as the lungs are to a human body, so is a park the breathing spot of the people, and if these efforts are successful, they will prove a lasting boon to the city of San Diego and a crown of glory to the Ladies Annex."

Simultaneously, development of the park proceeded at 25th and A streets adjacent to Golden Hill, then the city's poshest neighborhood. Mathias F. Heller, 29, who had just moved to San Diego from Missouri to join his father-in-law in a grocery store business, led the drive to build a playground, install plantings and lay out the park's first golf course. Golden Hill Park was the lushest section of Balboa Park for many years and it remains today a delight to nearby residents.

Kate Sessions moves in

Those meager beginnings prompted suggestions in 1890-91 to spend $5,000 annually on park improvements and to issue a $100,000 bond to build dams, lakes and boulevards. Kate Sessions, who had been overseeing the planting needs of the Hotel del Coronado, recommended that park planning get serious. She said Frederick Law Olmsted, the landscape architect of New York's Central Park, should get the job.

When the newly constituted Common Council (successor to the Board of Trustees) failed to act, Sessions took on the job herself. In 1892 she received a 10-year lease of 32 acres in the northwest corner of the park (Sixth Avenue at Upas Street). The council named her city gardener (with no salary) and required that she plant and maintain 100 "choice and varied sorts of trees" annually and provide 300 more "in park, street, plaza or school ground plantings."

Across from her Upas Street house, Sessions began cultivating trees for the city and plants for her customers. By the time her lease expired in 1903, she had turned the western edge of the park along Sixth Avenue into a lush demonstration of how the whole park might look. At its peak, her nursery contained about 20,000 plants, including experimental varieties never grown in the area. San Diegans began to see that their 1,400-acre "park" had potential!

"San Diego is so unique in her geographical position, so beautifully set on the hill slopes above the sea and so individual in her climate," Sessions told a public meeting in September 1899, "that we all need to be educated to the fact and keep it constantly in mind that this park of ours must not be like any other park in the United States. It can be different and individual because it is possible to be so, and it is not possible for others to pattern after it."

The Common Council should not have been surprised that Sessions' lease would prompt others to request equal treatment. The San Diego Agricultural Society requested 7.4 acres on which to hold the 1893 County Fair. The Naval National Guard Reserve sought land for a rifle range. Several businessmen wanted leases even more generous than that held by Sessions. One even boldly proposed to grow barley in the park. In July 1901, E.W. Scripps, owner of the *San Diego Sun* and Miramar Ranch, offered to donate enough trees and shrubs to landscape the entire park. The council once again considered selling off portions to finance improvements to the rest.

But most leasing and sales schemes were blocked. As Mayor D. C. Reed said in his annual message to the council in May 1897, "This 1,400 acres should for all time remain intact for this people and for their children's children, and be as sacred as Holy Writ; and whenever the financial condition of this city will justify, the same should be improved in a moderate manner; transforming her canyons into artificial lakes and serpentine drives; with roses, flowers and trees of all climes dotting her hillsides, making this park the grandest for scenery and beauty on the American continent, if not in the world."

Plans, Parsons and improvements

With city finances tight as ever, businessman Julius Wangenheim convinced the Chamber of Commerce in August 1902 to step in and form a Park Improvement Committee to oversee park planning and management until a formal park board was appointed in 1905.

The committee hired Mary B. Coulston, former editor of *Garden and Forest* magazine, as secretary and publicist. John McLaren, superintendent of Golden Gate Park, recommended the committee hire one of three landscape architects to prepare a master plan: the Olmsted Brothers (son and nephew of Frederick Law Olmsted Sr.), Warren H. Manning or Samuel Parsons Jr. George W. Marston, a

GEORGE W. MARSTON (1850-1946) CAME TO SAN DIEGO IN 1870, FOUNDED THE LEADING DEPARTMENT STORE, MARSTON'S, IN 1878 AND, AS SAN DIEGO'S "MERCHANT PRINCE" AND LEADING BENEFACTOR, HELPED FOUND MANY ORGANIZATIONS AND INSTITUTIONS, INCLUDING THE SAN DIEGO HISTORICAL SOCIETY. PARKS WERE ONE OF HIS MAJOR INTERESTS AND HE DEFENDED BALBOA PARK AGAINST UNWARRANTED INTRUSIONS. MARSTON POINT AT THE SOUTHWEST CORNER IS NAMED FOR HIM, AND HIS HOME ON SEVENTH AVENUE WAS INCORPORATED INTO THE PARK UPON THE DEATH OF HIS DAUGHTER, MARY MARSTON, WHO LIVED IN THE HOUSE UNTIL HER DEATH IN 1987.
San Diego Historical Society

POUND (CABRILLO) CANYON, C. 1903 IS NOW THE SITE OF STATE ROUTE 163. *San Diego Historical Society*

KATE SESSIONS SECURES 32-ACRE, 10-YEAR LEASE FOR NURSERY AT NORTHWEST CORNER.

1902

1892   SAMUEL PARSONS JR. HIRED TO PREPARE PARK PLAN; COMPLETED, 1905

EARLY ROAD CONSTRUCTION IN THE SOUTHWEST CORNER OF THE PARK, 1903 *San Diego Historical Society*

park committee member and now wealthy department store owner, offered to underwrite the master plan, estimated at $10,000. While on a business trip to New York, he retained Parsons' services. Marston told reporters when he returned that Parsons, the longtime superintendent of New York's Central Park and city park system, was "a businessman, artist and gardener, a rare combination."

Before his meeting with Marston, Parsons had corresponded with Coulston to review the prospects for working in San Diego. "I hope San Diego is disposed to spend a reasonable amount of money," he wrote, "for construction of parks is necessarily expensive, if it is done well, and it is not economical to do it poorly. I like all you say about the San Diego park, and I am sure a grand opportunity must exist there for a beautiful and most interesting park." Parsons arrived in San Diego December 21, 1902, for a 10-day reconnaissance. Marston gave him a grand tour of the area and in the *Union's* annual New Year's Day edition, he marveled at the park's potential:

"Every park has its own peculiar and more or less distinct characteristics, but this great area of spreading mesas and rugged, picturesque canyons is markedly different from all other parks I have seen in Europe and America... There is nothing like it among the parks of the world."

On his return to New York, Parsons began receiving sections of a contour map of the park on which to devise his plan. In March 1903 the chamber

committee hired John McLean, a Scottish botanist and surveyor and former foreman at San Francisco's Golden Gate Park. In April the council authorized its Board of Public Works to implement Parsons' plans. In May the first plan for roads and paths in the southwest area arrived, and Marston displayed it in his department store window at Fifth and C.

Foresters and Arbor Day celebrants

Enthusiasm spilled over into the fraternal orders of the Woodmen and Foresters. They announced they would plant the first 600 eucalyptus trees at the south end of the park. On July 4, 1903, 500 Foresters arrived by train from Los Angeles and joined a parade up Broadway, preceded by a brass band. After the speeches, only two Foresters showed up for the noon "planting" (just a ceremonial earth tamping) for one tree. So much for aid from L.A.

ARBOR DAY CELEBRATION, MARCH 17, 1904 *San Diego Historical Society*

The serious work began with the arrival later that month of George Cooke, Parsons' English partner. He oversaw the plowing, blasting of a hill near Sixth and Date, and the laying out of roads and paths before leaving for New York in August. Cooke returned for the winter (who wouldn't?) to supervise the grading of three miles of streets, planting of 1,000 trees and installation of a 7,000-foot irrigation system. The running total of park improvements through 1904 was $42,000, of which Marston donated about $31,000; his bank book indicated that he was reimbursed $23.

On March 17, 1904, about 2,500 school children participated in San Diego's first Arbor Day celebrations by planting 60 pines and cypresses on the west side of Pound Canyon (today's State Route 163). California Governor George Pardee said by telegram, "You could not do a better thing for your city, for yourselves and for those who come after you. The trees will live as long as you do and longer, and every year they will make San Diego more beautiful and inviting." President Theodore Roosevelt sent this message: "Your love of trees now will make you as men and women, lovers of forests, both for their natural beauty and economic value."

Mary Coulston left San Diego in April to resume her studies at the University of California at Berkeley and died unexpectedly July 18. She was cremated and her remains buried next to a cedar of Lebanon in the park.

OPENING OF ADAMS AVENUE STREETCAR LINE, 1907 *San Diego Historical Society*

A plan and money to carry it out

By year's end, Parsons was back in San Diego for a first-hand look. In a January 1, 1905, article in the *Union*, he praised growing enthusiasm for park improvements and foresaw what an asset the park would grow to become:

"Just think what an endowment for a city this park must remain. And as San Diego is and must be in the nature of things preeminently a tourist city, the existence of this scenery, which the park has done so much to bring within easy view as well as to give a worthy foreground to the picture, must continue to prove more and more a possible source of the finest enjoyment in those who visit California."

That same first month of 1905, city voters approved charter changes that authorized a park commission, appointed in April, and approved a special property tax of eight cents per $100 assessed valuation — $14,000 annually — dedicated to park improvements and maintenance.

By September Parsons delivered his report and plan. He envisioned a picturesque, naturalistic park — "a gem of solitude, unlike any other park in the world" — with winding roads, numerous gardens and preservation of the natural contours as much as possible to preserve views to the bay and mountains to the east. The canyons and "weird indentations of the surface of the earth" gave the park a distinct quality, he said, and they should not be interrupted by any building "that does not subserve the legitimate purpose for which the park was ordered." He recommended children's playgrounds, restrooms, lakes, roads, key entrances and police patrols.

"To know what not to do, and when to stop, is about the last thing an artist learns," he concluded, "and not many ever learn it at all, only the great ones, perhaps. In the matter of public parks there are so many of the public to whom it belongs, who, being unable to comprehend for just what purpose it was made, try constantly, and with good intentions, to divert it to uses altogether apart from the original and true purpose of it, that constant pressure of sane public opinion is needed to save it from them." He ended by hoping that San Diegans would keep the park "forever free from the interjection of all foreign, extraneous and hurtful purposes or objects."

Nolen adds an idea

Over the next four years, some of those "extraneous and hurtful" elements already in the park disappeared — the rifle clubs and unsightly squatters' shacks. Annual plantings slowly filled in the western edge of the park much as Parsons had specified. Proposals for five schools and a firehouse were rejected. George Cooke, Parsons' assistant who moved permanently to San Diego in 1907 to oversee the park and act as county road engineer, died in a road accident near Alpine and was replaced in 1909 by Los Angeles landscape architect Wilbur D. Cook. Parsons returned in 1910 to prepare a citywide park plan. "The park is not a botanical garden or experimental station," he wrote, "but a spot of great natural beauty, which it is desired to make accessible by roads and paths, and to ornament with trees and shrubs in the most economical and effective manner possible."

The enthusiastic support of Parsons' plan led to Marston's next planning effort, the preparation of a master plan for the entire city. Again acting from a chamber committee, this one called the Civic Improvement Committee, Marston hired Cambridge, Massachusetts, landscape architect John Nolen, a nationally known pioneer in city planning. Completed in 1908, the Nolen Plan called for extending the park's western boundary one block west to secure a prominent view toward the bay. His boldest concept was a 12-block, bay-park link between Date and Elm streets, from Fifth Avenue to the waterfront.

"The people of San Diego," Nolen wrote, "would do well if they recognize today the two great central recreation features of the city, now and always, are the City Park of 1,400 acres and the bayfront, and that the value of both will be increased many-fold if a suitable connecting link, parkway or boulevard, can be developed, bringing them into direct and pleasant relation. Here, on this hillside, at comparatively small expense, can be developed what I have called, after the custom in Spanish and Spanish-American cities, 'The Paseo,' a pleasant promenade, an airing place, a formal and dignified approach to the big central park, free from railroad grade crossings.

"At the waterfront the Paseo would spread out to a width of 1,200 feet, and in this perfectly splendid situation, commanding the grandeur of San Diego's most characteristic scenery, the people could establish the proposed casino, art museum and aquarium, surrounding them with the lovely parks and gardens, which only the climatic conditions of Southern California make possible."

SAILORS FROM THE GREAT WHITE FLEET MARCHING TOWARD THE PARK, 1908
San Diego Historical Society

The cost to buy the land and cross the railroad tracks perhaps doomed Nolen's vision. But the civic dream of linking bay and park never remained long out of the public debate over how to shape San Diego's future.

Some businessmen thought it took too much time and money to implement Parsons' plan. With the construction of the Panama Canal well under way, San Diego civic leaders imagined that their destiny lay in developing a vital port to serve ships heading to and from Central America. They set aside Parsons' plans and Nolen's dreams, but they found a useful role for City Park in their game plan for the 20th century.

SITE OF BALBOA STADIUM PRIOR TO CONSTRUCTION, 1914 *San Diego Historical Society*

DOWNTOWN SAN DIEGO FROM MARSTON POINT *Photo by Robert A. Eplett, Inset San Diego Historical Society*

FIFTH AVENUE NEAR G STREET *Photo by Robert A. Eplett, 1999, Inset, c.1888 San Diego Historical Society*

SIXTH AVENUE AND CEDAR *Photo by Robert A. Eplett, Inset San Diego Historical Society*

1906

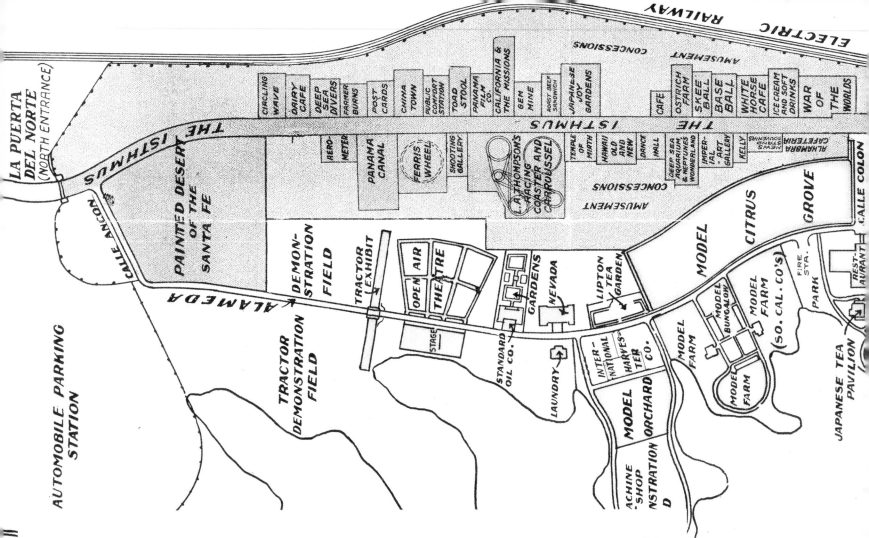

INDEX
TO
GROUND PLAN MAP

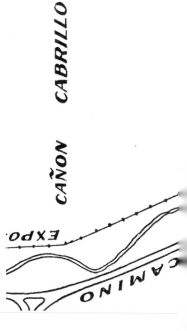

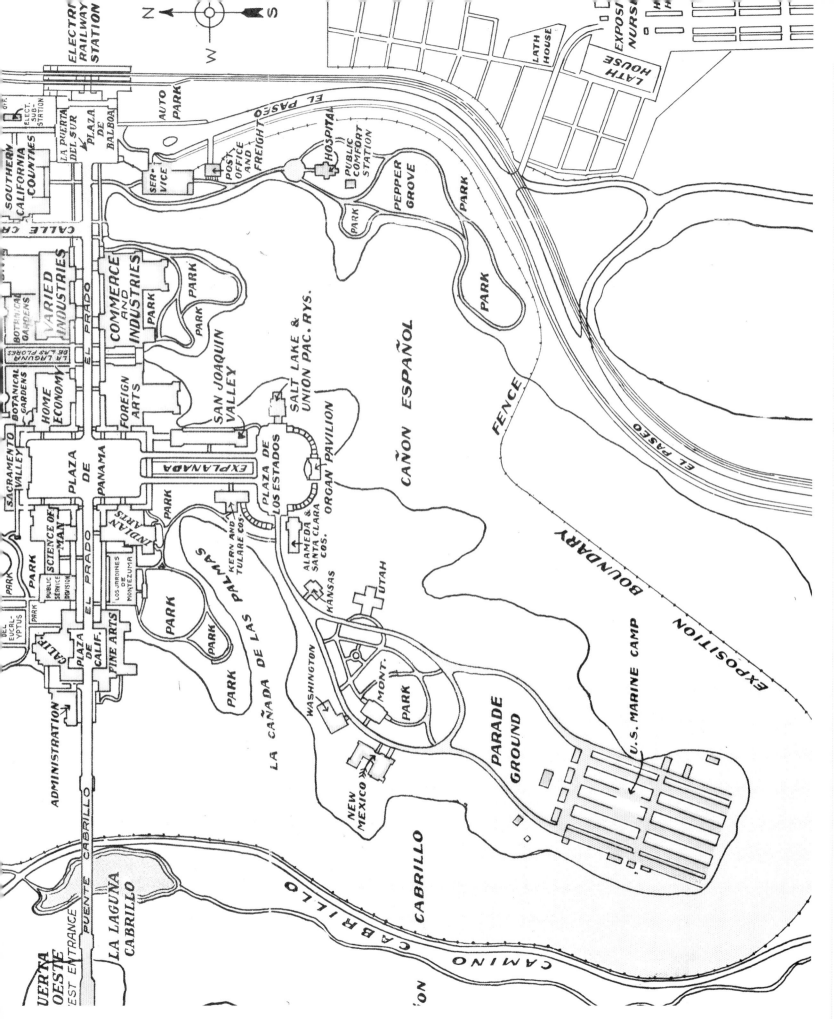

MAP OF THE PANAMA-CALIFORNIA EXPOSITION, 1915 *San Diego Historical Society*

A Splendid Pleasure Ground
1909 — 1945

Chapter Two

"All in all, the wilderness of the naked mesas and canyons of cactus and coyotes has in some magical way become a fairy city of palaces and playgrounds, a public school of the arts and a splendid pleasure ground of gardens, lawns, forested spaces and charming driveways. It is today one of the notable parks of the country."

— George W. Marston, 1936

Shortly before midnight on December 31, 1914, San Diegans and visitors gathered in Balboa Park's Plaza de Panama in anticipation of a momentous event, the official opening of the nearly $5 million Panama-California Exposition. In just five years, a featureless mesa had become a "magic city" of wondrous palaces filled with fabulous treasures. The grounds were planted with thousands of quick-blooming flowers, shrubs and trees.

Awakened just before 3 a.m. Washington time, President Woodrow Wilson touched a Western Union telegraph button, sending a signal that the lights should go on and the fair begin. On the roof of the Spreckels Organ Pavilion, a fireworks display in the shape of a ship, the "1915," started through a model of the Panama Canal. "Before the lights had dimmed," the *Union* reported, "letters broke through the mass of shooting flame, which read, 'The land divided — the world united — San Diego, the first port of call.'"

A series of speakers that night and the next day predicted this grand event would change the course of San Diego's history. As Mayor Charles F. O'Neall put it, "...from this summit the future,

bright as the millennial dawn, stretches before us and in the dim distance we see San Diego of our dreams — the metropolis of the great West, the star of cities, built by love and labor upon the foundation stones of location, harbor, climate, soil and Exposition."

It all began with a suggestion on July 9, 1909, by G. Aubrey Davidson, newly elected president of the Chamber of Commerce. He said San Diego could mark the opening of the Panama Canal with a world's fair and thereby give the local economy a lift and draw attention to San Diego's potential as a superb port.

With a population of about 50,000, San Diego was the smallest city, before or since, ever to host a fair of this kind. To have pressed forward despite major political and financial roadblocks showed incredible faith in the city's future. San Diego, said one booster, was "the pluckiest, nerviest and gamest city in the United States and probably the world."

Within weeks, exposition fever gripped the city. Businessmen pledged thousands of dollars to bankroll the effort. City Park was chosen as the site, although San Diego's leading architect, Irving J. Gill, among other critics, said better locations to highlight San

AN AIRPLANE FLIES OVER THE MODEL FARM PRIOR TO THE OPENING OF THE EXPOSITION, 1914. *San Diego Historical Society*

Diego's maritime potential would be on North Island or Point Loma. A few dissenters threw cold water on the whole idea. Former Judge Alfred Haines said the money would be better spent on permanent civic improvements. "It is time somebody spoke out against the proposed extravagance," he said.

But such voices were drowned out by undisguised boosterism. "The Panama-California Exposition at San Diego — 'The Southwest Gate' — in 1915!" the *Union* trumpeted on the front page. "Paste that in your hat — paste it on the walls of your office — paste it on your business stationery — paste it where it will stick for years! Then talk exposition — sing exposition — boost exposition — and it will be a go. San Diego wants it — San Diego needs it — and San Diego will have it. But it is up to you. You must do your share."

Politics, site and design

Before San Diego could get things rolling, it faced a rival fair proposed at the same time by San Francisco, a city 10 times bigger and eager to demonstrate to the world that it had risen from the ashes of its 1906 earthquake and fire. Ultimately, San Diego agreed to hold a smaller fair with exhibits from Latin America, California counties and whichever states could be persuaded to send them. San Francisco then was free to stage a truly world's fair, the Panama-Pacific International Exposition, to which the president of the United States formally invited all nations to send displays and delegations.

Politics may have figured in the decision. President William Howard Taft had a personal connection to San Diego; he had visited the city twice and his parents and sister had moved here. But Taft faced a tough reelection bid in 1912 and needed California's electoral votes. When D.C. "Charlie" Collier, the first director-general of the San Diego fair, sought some of the $5 million set aside to celebrate the Panama Canal's opening, Congress instead sent money to San Francisco. Collier blamed Taft for sidetracking a Senate bill recognizing San Diego's fair but he lacked proof of collusion. "To hell with Congress," he fumed. "San Diego has raised $3 million on her own; we won't fight over the lousy $5 million. We'll have our own fair."

If Taft favored San Francisco, it did him no good politically. He didn't even appear on the California ballot. The state went for former President Theodore Roosevelt, running as a Progressive. San Diego voted for the winner, Woodrow Wilson, a Democrat.

The next challenge was to raise money and settle on a site and design. By March 1910 private pledges surpassed $1 million and in August, voters approved an equal amount in bonds by a seven-to-one margin, followed by an additional $850,000 in 1913 (carried by a 16-1 margin). The state granted $250,000 for the California Tower building (home today of the Museum of Man). At first, the San

Diego Exposition Company hoped to hire Daniel Burnham, architect for the trend-setting 1893 World's Columbian Exposition in Chicago. When he declined, they turned to the Olmsted Brothers of Brookline, Massachusetts. They were given a site in City Park, just north of San Diego High School.

John C. and Frederick Law Olmsted Jr., who had lost the 1902 park planning contract to Parsons, were promised a $15,000 fee and promptly began working out the fair's components. But their plan remained on paper. Exposition directors suddenly shifted the site to Vizcaíno Mesa (now called Central Mesa, the Prado area). Why? John D. Spreckels, San Diego's most powerful businessman who owned the *Union* and *Evening Tribune*, North Island, the Hotel del Coronado and many other enterprises, may have seen an opportunity to extend his streetcar system through the park and on to University Heights where he maintained Mission Cliff Gardens. Researcher Gregory Montes suspects that Spreckels withheld payment on his $100,000 pledge to the exposition until the site was to his liking.

The official reason given for changing the location was to reduce expenses by building on level ground. But this site, the Olmsteds believed, would compromise the park as a landscaped oasis by constructing exhibit halls right in the center. John C. Olmsted submitted his firm's resignation, warning park Commissioner Julius Wangenheim in a telegram:

"Exposition would be somewhat more grandiose there but that gain would not justify ruining park, would cost more there because of bridge [extending Laurel Street across the State Route 163 canyon], would not take in nearly as much there for gate money and concessions, especially in the evening, would not advertise city and harbor as well by close and full view [at the southern site] and would leave permanent buildings in remote and unsuitable place, especially for evening entertainments."

Olmsted prepared preliminary plans and estimates, which may or may not have been followed. In any case, one lasting change was to complete the western edge of the park by extending Sixth Avenue across Mulvey Canyon between Date and Juniper streets. James Mulvey had laid out paths, plantings and other features in the canyon, and his neighbors won a restraining order to keep the city from filling the canyon and building the street. In 1913 a court dissolved the order and construction proceeded. Once the street went through, the old name for Sixth Avenue north of Juniper, Park Avenue, vanished.

Conspicuously absent from exposition planning and early boosterism was George Marston. He had favored the Olmsted plan but was outvoted by the exposition board of directors. He resigned from the Buildings and Grounds Committee and left on an extended trip to Europe. His only official role thereafter was to head a commission overseeing the design and construction of the California

G. AUBREY DAVIDSON (1868-1957) WAS BORN IN CANADA, CAME TO SAN DIEGO TO WORK FOR THE RAILROAD AND LATER BECAME A SUCCESSFUL BANKER AND REAL ESTATE DEVELOPER. AS PRESIDENT OF THE CHAMBER OF COMMERCE IN 1909, HE PROPOSED THE PANAMA-CALIFORNIA EXPOSITION AND LATER HEADED THE COMMITTEE OVERSEEING THE 1935-36 CALIFORNIA PACIFIC INTERNATIONAL EXPOSITION.
San Diego Historical Society

D.C. "CHARLIE" COLLIER (1871-1934), LAWYER, DEVELOPER, WELL-LIKED SAN DIEGO BOOSTER, WAS DIRECTOR-GENERAL OF THE FIRST FAIR. HE CHOSE THE SITE AND SET THE DESIGN AND THEME. HE LATER WAS INVOLVED IN WORLD'S FAIRS IN BRAZIL, PHILADELPHIA AND CHICAGO.
San Diego Historical Society

GROUNDBREAKING CEREMONY FOR THE PANAMA-CALIFORNIA EXPOSITION, 1911 — THE $5 MILLION FAIR OPENED ON TIME FOUR YEARS LATER. *San Diego Historical Society*

Building and tower in the park. Frederick Law Olmsted Jr. would return to Balboa Park in 1947 to advise the city again.

Not only did the exposition directors switch land planners, they also replaced their lead architect, San Diego's Irving J. Gill. Gill had been the natural choice because of his expertise in Mission Revival architecture, the theme chosen to emphasize San Diego's Hispanic roots and to mark a radical break from the traditional choice of Roman and Greek classical styles for such fairs. But behind-the-scenes lobbying from various parties led to hiring a more prominent name, Bertram G. Goodhue, a New York architect known for his work in the more decorative Spanish Colonial Revival style. "I consider myself quite a shark on the sort of stuff they ought to have and am pretty familiar with Californian conditions," he wrote a supporter. Gill resigned after apparently working

on the first exposition building, the Administration Building at the eastern end of the Cabrillo Bridge. The exposition's look and legacy — and the future course of Southern California architecture — would no doubt have been quite different if Gill, rather than Goodhue, had remained in charge.

A new name and festive start

In November 1910 the Park Commission did what a number of residents and visitors had urged earlier. They gave City Park a more notable name. Samuel Parsons Jr., when he updated his park plans that year, had suggested naming the park after Cabrillo, the European who discovered San Diego in 1542. A number of suggestions appeared in local newspapers and later accounts credit Pioneer Society member Harriet Phillips with the ultimate selection,

GROUNDBREAKING CEREMONY FOR 1915 PANAMA-CALIFORNIA EXPOSITION, 1911 *San Diego Historical Society*

QUEEN RAMONA (HELENE RICHARDS) ON PARADE FLOAT DURING THE GROUNDBREAKING FESTIVAL FOR THE 1915 EXPOSITION, 1911 *San Diego Historical Society*

Balboa Park. The selection was an apt one. Spanish conquistador Vasco Núñez de Balboa was the first European to see the Pacific Ocean as he led an expedition across the Isthmus of Panama in 1513. "It is a harsh-sounding name," objected state Senator W.W. Bowers. "One must make an effort to pronounce it: must fix his mouth to do it. It is wholly wanting of any suggestion of a pleasant character." But Balboa Park it was.

A great festival, July 16-19, 1911, culminated in a glorious groundbreaking ceremony. Construction began under the direction of Frank P. Allen Jr., who had managed the 1909 Alaska-Yukon Pacific Exposition in Seattle. The 1,505-foot-long Cabrillo Bridge, California's first multi-arched, cantilevered span, connected the Central Mesa to the already-landscaped Sixth Avenue strip. The 200-foot California Tower rose skyward, a new and lasting landmark for the hopeful city.

Along the central east-west avenue called El Prado, Goodhue, his assistant Carleton Winslow and other associate architects and skillful artisans created a series of stunning palaces. The buildings

continued on page 58

American Indian workers with shovels at the park during the construction of the 1915 exposition, 1914 *San Diego Historical Society*

BUILDING CONSTRUCTION ALONG BALBOA PARK'S "MAIN STREET" EL PRADO, 1913 *San Diego Historical Society*

CALIFORNIA TOWER CONSTRUCTION WITH BOTANICAL GARDEN AND MODEL FARM IN FOREGROUND, C. 1914 *San Diego Historical Society*

VIEW OF SAN DIEGO FROM BALBOA PARK, 1915 *Andreas Brown Postcard Collection, San Diego Historical Society*

SAN DIEGO VIEWS FOR PANAMA-CALIFORNIA EXPOSITION, 1915 *Andreas Brown Postcard Collection, San Diego Historical Society*

Fanciful interpretation of what the Panama-California Exposition would look like, by A. J. Roberts for the San Diego Decorating Company, 1913
San Diego Historical Society

SAN DIEGO
1916
EXPOSITION

DEDICATION
MARCH 18TH

NEW INTERNATIONAL
EXPOSITION

WESTERN LITHOGRAPH CO. LOS ANGELES CAL.

Dedication poster for the revised 1916 Panama-California International Exposition *San Diego Historical Society*

Aerial view of Balboa Park and surrounding residential areas of San Diego, 1915 *San Diego Historical Society*

EXPOSITION CROWD ENTERS THE PARK OVER THE CABRILLO BRIDGE, 1915 *San Diego Historical Society*

SPEAKER OF THE U.S. HOUSE OF REPRESENTATIVES, JOSEPH G. CANNON, ALONGSIDE JOHN D. SPRECKELS (WITH HAT ON HEAD) IN AN ELECTRIQUETTE CART, 1915 *San Diego Historical Society*

CHILDREN WITH KELLOGG'S CORN FLAKES BOXES TIED AROUND THEIR NECKS AT EXPOSITION, 1915 *San Diego Historical Society*

EDGAR L. HEWETT
(1865-1946)
WAS DIRECTOR OF
AMERICAN RESEARCH AT
THE ARCHAEOLOGICAL
INSTITUTE OF AMERICA AND
FOUNDER OF THE SCHOOL
OF AMERICAN RESEARCH IN
SANTA FE, NEW MEXICO. HE
SERVED AS DIRECTOR OF
EXHIBITS IN SCIENCE AND
ART FOR THE PANAMA-
CALIFORNIA EXPOSITION
AND FOUNDED AND HEADED
THE SAN DIEGO MUSEUM
(RENAMED MUSEUM OF
MAN IN 1942) UNTIL 1929.
San Diego Historical Society

THE INDIAN VILLAGE IN THE PAINTED DESERT OF THE SANTA FE EXHIBIT, 1915 *San Diego Historical Society*

looked as solid as a stone cathedral but in reality were box-shaped barns whose decorations were simply plaster and hemp meant to last only a few years. Park Superintendent John Morley laid out the plantings on the exposition periphery, while Allen supervised the construction of streets and grounds with the assistance of Paul Thiene, a San Diego nurseryman. Hundreds of workers lived in four-man bunkhouses and had their bruises tended at a 26-patient hospital.

When the public finally got to see the result in January 1915, the effect was overwhelming and far-reaching. Goodhue had so captured the romance of Old Spain and Mexico that Southern California experienced a widespread revival of Spanish Colonial architecture. As one newspaper article rightly foretold, "[Spanish Colonial] architecture is destined to take on new life and strength and to last for many years to come."

Some architects blamed the craze for retarding innovative American architecture for 20 years. But Frank Lloyd Wright, the nation's leading modern architect at the time and occasional visitor to San Diego, gave one of his rare compliments for another architect's work. "I think the park is delightful," Wright said in the 1955 speech. "I drove through it today and was delighted with what has remained. Bertram Goodhue happened to be a good man. I don't see how he got the job to build that fair. But he did!

I don't know why it is that good things are controversial items and the better they are, seemingly, the more controversial they are. I take that comfort to myself."

A new twist

The 640-acre Panama-California Exposition was different from San Francisco's Panama-Pacific and other fairs in several ways besides architectural style. Exhibits were designed to demonstrate how products were manufactured. For a 50-cent admission (25 cents for children), fairgoers could visit a working film studio, inspect the Lipton Tea Company's tea plantation and study anthropology, based on excavations carried out around the world by the Smithsonian Institution's Alex Hrdlicka and the Archaeological Institute of America, headed by Edgar L. Hewett. At the "Painted Desert of the Santa Fe," 300 Native Americans from New Mexico occupied a village and trading post, demonstrating daily life at home. Many visitors got around the fairgrounds by means of two-person "electriquettes," battery-powered, golf-cart sized vehicles available for rent.

Seven states were represented at the fair: California, Kansas, Montana, Nevada, New Mexico, Utah and Washington. Of California's 58 counties, 28 exhibited in five buildings. No foreign countries were present in 1915 but there were exhibits of Brazilian

continued on page 70

Leap Year Court during the exposition — romantic gardens and lush landscaping were key design components of the fair. *San Diego Historical Society*

Japanese Tea Pavilion with teahouse, stream and bridge located behind the Botanical Building, 1915; the children's zoo replaced it in 1957. *San Diego Historical Society*

THE $100,000 SPRECKELS ORGAN PAVILION, 1915, DESIGNED BY HARRISON ALBRIGHT WAS DONATED BY JOHN AND ADOLPH SPRECKELS, THE SONS OF THE HAWAIIAN SUGAR KING. THE SPRECKELS COMPANIES UNDERWROTE THE ORGANIST'S SALARY UNTIL 1929. *San Diego Historical Society*

FORMAL GARDENS AND CITRUS ORCHARD WITH ROLLER COASTER IN THE BACKGROUND, 1915

Andreas Brown Postcard Collection, San Diego Historical Society

SOUVENIR MONEY FROM THE LUCK OF FORTY NINE ROARING CAMP GOLD MINING ATTRACTION ON THE ISTHMUS, 1915

San Diego Historical Society

EX-PRESIDENT WILLIAM HOWARD TAFT AND G. AUBREY DAVIDSON AT THE EXPOSITION, 1915 *San Diego Historical Society*

FORMER PRESIDENT THEODORE ROOSEVELT (CENTER) ADDRESSED NAVY CADETS AT THE EXPOSITION WITH GEORGE W. MARSTON (1ST FROM LEFT) AND GEORGE BURNHAM (2ND FROM LEFT) JULY 30, 1915. *San Diego Historical Society*

ARRIVAL OF THE LIBERTY BELL AT THE EXPOSITION, NOVEMBER 12, 1915 *San Diego Historical Society*

Human Navy pennant in
Plaza de Panama during
the exposition, 1915
San Diego Historical Society

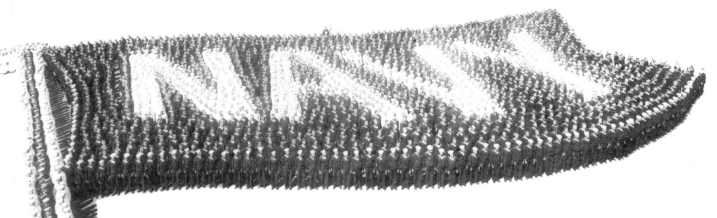

John D. Spreckels
(1853-1926),
newspaper owner and
railroad magnate who
donated $100,000 for
construction of the
organ pavilion in the
park, c. 1911
San Diego Historical Society

coffee and a traditional Japanese tea pavilion. (At the San Francisco fair were exhibits from 28 states and U.S. territories and 22 nations.)

Military and music were big at the San Diego fair. The 1st U.S. Cavalry and a Marine Corps unit, living at a model camp, put on military programs. John D. Spreckels and his brother Adolph paid for the $100,000 outdoor organ and pavilion and underwrote daily concerts. A favorite performer was Ernestine Schumann-Heink, the world's greatest contralto, who made her home in San Diego. Gertrude Gilbert, who oversaw the exposition's music program, would later play a leading role in saving the exposition buildings. Women indeed played major roles in exposition activities, and that

wasn't by accident. Alice Klauber and her fellow members of the San Diego County Women's Association threatened to disseminate bad publicity if they did not win special services and programs for women who visited the fair.

Fair publicists made much of the fact that this would be a year-round event and toward the end of 1915, directors raised additional funds from Los Angeles businessmen to carry on for a second year. Many exhibits were shipped from the closed San Francisco fair to the renamed Panama-California International Exposition. New exhibits came from Brazil, Canada, France, Germany, the Netherlands, Spain and Switzerland, some because the outbreak of World War I

Ernestine
Schumann-Heink
(1851-1936),
popular opera singer
who resided part-time in
San Diego and performed
during both expositions.
San Diego Historical Society

Marine parade through the Plaza de Panama, 1915 *San Diego Historical Society*

HAWAIIAN VILLAGE HULA DANCERS AT THE "HAWAII OLD AND NEW" EXHIBIT, 1915 *San Diego Historical Society*

prevented them from returning to Europe. Dedicated March 18, 1916, the extended fair gave new names to several buildings to reflect the new exhibits.

There also were new attractions at the most popular section of the fair, the fun zone called "The Isthmus." In addition to the usual freak shows, games of chance and amusement park rides was a diorama, the "War of the Worlds." As explained in the official fair guide, the story line involved an adventurer named Rabinoff who leads an alliance of nations from Asia and Africa on a frightening invasion of New York in the year 2000:

"The designer of the extravaganza also figures that there will be interplanetary communication, and so, in addition to the ships of the world nations, he introduces the aerial fleets from Mars and other planets. The principal part of the extravaganza is the naval battle in New York harbor and the aerial battle overhead. The concession is probably the most complete thing of the sort ever attempted, with remarkable features as the control of some of the ships by wireless apparatus and the use of 11 miles of electric wire for control of other pieces of mechanism in the production. There are large motors and there are tiny motors which can be held in the hand."

San Diego's fair officially ended January 1, 1917, but the fairgrounds continued on an admission-only basis for three more months as exhibitors dismantled their attractions and officials began the task of deciding what to do with the magic city that had reshaped Balboa Park and put San Diego on the map. Attendance had totaled 2,050,030 in 1915 and 1,697,886 in 1916, and yielded a surplus of $34,000. (San Francisco's fair drew 18,876,438 during its 10-month run and produced a $2,401,931 surplus.) Former presidents (Theodore Roosevelt and William Howard Taft) and a future president (Franklin D. Roosevelt) had attended. Thomas Edison and Henry Ford came on the same day. The Liberty Bell from Philadelphia made an appearance. So did art works by Monet, Degas and Rodin. There were frequent military demonstrations and exhibits of fine art. This undoubtedly was the most exciting two years in San Diego's history. And out of it came a fully landscaped and cherished grand urban park. Surely, designs on parkland for nonpark purposes were at an end. But that was not to be.

The park goes to war

Months before the exposition closed, there were many calls for retaining the buildings for new purposes, even though they were designed to last no more than two or three years. Ideas included a military academy, university campus or civic center. Businessman John F. Forward Jr., among many farsighted leaders, quelled such

continued on page 76

Tents and sailors at the park during World War I along Park Boulevard, 1917-1918 *San Diego Historical Society*

ARMISTICE DAY PARADE THROUGH THE PARK, NOVEMBER 11, 1921 *San Diego Historical Society*

Aerial view of the Plaza de Panama and the Spreckels Organ Pavilion, 1921 — after World War I San Diegans lobbied to keep the exposition buildings rather than raze them as was originally intended. *San Diego Historical Society*

talk. "This plan of locating county and city buildings at the exposition is bunk, piffle and slush," Forward said in July 1916. "That park was set aside for use of the people and it was specifically stated it was to be used for park purposes only."

All talk of reuse ended when Congress declared war on Germany April 6, 1917, and newly elected Mayor Louis J. Wilde (who had defeated George Marston April 3) offered the fairgrounds for military purposes. The Navy proceeded to occupy all buildings and grounds east of the Plaza de Panama and the city spent almost $30,000 to alter the buildings for military use. By year's end more than 5,000 recruits were training in the park The Navy men drilled in the Plaza de Panama, ate outside in the courtyard of the Cafe Cristóbal and slept in tents north of the Southern Counties Building (future site of the Natural History Museum). "Clad in white duck uniforms," the *Union* reported in June 1917, "the 1,000 youths at the naval training camp offer an inspiring sight at their daily drills,

especially during the morning setting-up exercises and during battalion and regimental maneuvers."

For amusement, the rest of the park was kept busy with events for both military and civilians. Katherine Tingley, head of the Theosophical Society on Point Loma, offered to put on plays in an open-air theater. There were requests to set up a roller-skating rental stand and construction of a swimming pool in a canyon. The San Diego Public Library opened a branch in the Indian Arts Building (House of Charm). It didn't take long for accidents (and pranks) to occur. The park commissioners wrote the commanding officer in October that "a party of men in uniform" was seen overturning a large ornamental urn at about 1:15 a.m. and that ornamental light globes had been broken from the tops of standards in the same area.

In May 1918, the park board granted the Marine Corps permission to occupy several buildings around the Spreckels Organ Pavilion on condition that it "not disturb any trees, plants, shrubs or lawns or make any changes of any nature in the area adjacent to said buildings, erect any building, dig any trenches or in any manner disturb the grounds... without the full knowledge, consent and written support of this board or its superintendent of parks."

As the park went to war, the remaining exposition buildings and grounds found new uses. Concerts continued unabated at the Spreckels Organ Pavilion. Special civic and sporting events took place at Balboa Stadium. Two institutions grew out of the fair — the San Diego Museum (which went on to spawn the Museum of Man, Museum of Art and other institutions) and the San Diego Zoo.

The California Quadrangle, built as a permanent structure, was turned over to the newly established San Diego Museum, directed by Edgar L. Hewett, overseer of the fair's educational and scientific exhibits. The California Building and Tower became the Museum of Ancient America. The Science and Education Building just to the east held Indian arts and crafts. The Indian Arts Building (House of Charm) became an anthropology building. The Fine Arts Building (opposite the California Tower) continued as an art gallery. And the Sacramento Valley Building (later site of the San Diego Museum of Art) held Joseph Jessop's archery collection. Museum dues were $5 for corporations, $2 for students, teachers and artists. "The Museum of San Diego is already the largest west of Chicago," Hewett wrote in the *Union*. "The buildings that have been granted for its use may be conservatively valued at half a million dollars; the collections on exhibition or in process of installation at a quarter of a million." And new exhibits and collections were constantly added. For example, Ellen Browning Scripps, who had supported the Egypt Exploration Society, saw to it that

some of the surplus artifacts found at ancient Egyptian sites went to the San Diego Museum.

A roaring start

A zoo had long been talked about and promoted for Balboa Park. An aviary had been built on Sixth Avenue and deer and sundry wild animals were displayed in makeshift cages in the same area. During the fair, there were five mini-zoos in the park. No one apparently thought of combining them into one institution until the idea came to Dr. Harry Wegeforth, who with his brother was an official surgeon at the exposition. As Wegeforth recalled later, on September 16, 1916, he heard the roar of exposition lions as he drove toward the park and turned to his brother Paul, saying, "Wouldn't it be splendid if San Diego had a zoo! You know — I think I'll start one."

He proceeded to *The San Diego Union* offices downtown and laid out his dream to City Editor Clarence McGrew, who published the proposal the next day. A board was formed two weeks later and articles of incorporation were filed in Sacramento in November. The motley assortment of animals then in the park was brought together with the menagerie at the defunct Wonderland amusement park in Ocean Beach. Since the 1920s, donations from children and their parents, businesses and major donors have built the institution into one of the world's best and most innovative.

With peace declared on November 11, 1918, the military left the park for permanent bases around San Diego Bay and the race was on

DR. HARRY WEGEFORTH (1882-1941), SURGEON AT THE PANAMA-CALIFORNIA EXPOSITION, FOUNDED THE SAN DIEGO ZOO IN 1916 AND CHAMPIONED ITS GROWTH FOR ITS FIRST 25 YEARS, OFTEN ENLISTING THE AID OF THE CITY'S CHILDREN IN HIS VARIOUS CAMPAIGNS. *San Diego Historical Society*

CAST MEMBERS BEING HANDED RIFLES FOR THE FILMING OF *The American* IN THE PLAZA DE PANAMA, C. 1920 *San Diego Historical Society*

WILLIAM TEMPLETON
JOHNSON
(1877-1957),
ARCHITECT OF THE FINE
ARTS GALLERY (LATER SAN
DIEGO MUSEUM OF ART)
AND THE SAN DIEGO
NATURAL HISTORY
MUSEUM, C. 1930
San Diego Historical Society

ELLEN BROWNING SCRIPPS
(1836-1932),
PROMINENT
PHILANTHROPIST, DONATED
$125,000 TOWARD THE
CONSTRUCTION OF THE
SAN DIEGO NATURAL
HISTORY MUSEUM, 1923.
San Diego Historical Society

to use the exposition buildings rather than demolish them. The Boy Scouts occupied the Indian Village. The Southern Counties building became the Civic Auditorium. A new golf course was built on the East Mesa and the County Fair began holding annual showings in September 1919, utilizing various exposition buildings. City officials rejected proposals for a movie studio, but the park starred as the backdrop for several films including Allan Dwan's *Soldiers of Fortune* in the Plaza de Panama in May 1919.

Proposals regularly surfaced to sell off pieces of the park to raise money for other city purposes. "The sale of 500 acres of that park would hasten our town along 18 years," Mayor Wilde said. "It is a regular sucker play for us to have that big park up there creating nothing but a big expense." One letter writer, H. J. Penfold, argued that instead of cutting down the park, San Diego should present itself to the state as one big year-round playground and a hometown for hundreds of millionaires. "The first thing to do is plan some great permanent attraction," he said. "That would be our wonderful park, with its exposition of everything that has to do with the history and development of the state of California. What a wealth of material there is to work on there. No other state in the Union has so much to offer." Instead, city voters deeded land for a permanent Naval Hospital complex at Inspiration Point and for (Theodore) Roosevelt Junior High School at Park Boulevard and Upas Street.

Mere stage scenery

Of more immediate concern was the state of the exposition buildings, which architect Bertram Goodhue and colleagues had planned to last only through 1916. It was now 1920 and cost estimates upwards of $1 million were advanced for keeping the buildings intact. In 1922 the park board asked Bertram Goodhue for his advice. "We know it is entirely contrary to your convictions that the buildings should be retained," Thomas N. Faulconer, the board's executive secretary wrote, "but they have been retained and now the people refuse to part with them."

Goodhue replied that the nonpermanent buildings were "mere stage scenery" and "structurally, of the flimsiest sort," continuing, "They are now crumbling, disintegrating and altogether unlovely structures, structures that lack any of the venerability of age and present only its pathos, and the space they occupy could readily be made into one of the most beautiful public gardens in the New World."

By 1924 more than $140,000 had been raised to restore 17 buildings. Project manager G. Edward Chase predicted the repairs would add 20 years to the buildings' lives. (It would take another 75 years and tens of millions of dollars to finish the job.) Park Commissioner Hugo Klauber reported that lack of money hindered landscaping improvements. "Many trees have died and many have been removed," he said in a report in the *Union*, "and literally hundreds have blown down because of insufficient root formation, caused by faulty planting during the rush of preparing for our exposition. This is very costly economy and should never be repeated." He advocated a 40-50 percent increase in property tax support for all city parks.

In two instances, private donations made possible the replacement rather than restoration of exposition buildings. Appleton and Amelia Bridges donated more than $400,000 to build the Fine Arts Gallery (renamed the San Diego Museum of Art in 1978). Located at the prime spot on the north side of the Plaza de Panama, the art gallery with 10,000 square feet of exhibit space was designed by William Templeton Johnson and opened February 28, 1926. Mrs. Bridges was the daughter of wealthy industrialist Henry H. Timken, inventor of the roller bearing. The Timken family would later figure in the construction of the Timken Museum of Art nearby.

The other major donation in the 1920s came from Ellen Browning Scripps, half-sister of newspaper magnate E.W. Scripps. Miss Scripps gave $125,000 for a permanent Natural History Museum building. The San Diego Society of Natural History, founded in 1874, was the city's oldest scientific-cultural institution and was outgrowing the exposition buildings it briefly occupied. Also designed by William Templeton Johnson, the new building opened on January 15, 1933. It occupied the site of the Southern Counties Building, which had become the Civic Auditorium after the war. It was destroyed by fire November 25, 1925, just hours before the scheduled start of the annual firemen's ball. An overheated furnace was blamed. The naturalists got a 60,000-square-foot museum but conventioneers and major meeting planners would have to wait until 1989 to get a full-fledged facility, the San Diego Convention Center, capable of accommodating major national conventions and trade shows.

Joseph W. Sefton Jr., banker and president of the Society of Natural History, shed no tears for the Civic Auditorium. "All those old exposition buildings are nothing but fire traps," he said. "They are a real menace. The people here are living in a sort of fool's paradise. We think we have something in the park that is beautiful and of which we can be proud. In reality we have some houses of tinder. They are pretty to look at, but we may wake up any morning and find them gone, and our million dollars worth of exhibits with them."

One other park addition in this period remains one of the most beloved. A Herschell-Spillman carousel, built in North Tonawanda, New York, first operated in 1910 in Los Angeles' Luna Park and then was sold to H.D. Simpson, an Englishman who moved it in 1914 to Coronado's Tent City resort, southeast of the Hotel del Coronado. He may have moved it back and forth between Coronado and Balboa Park before installing it permanently in the park in March 1922, just south of the Plaza de Balboa (present site of the Reuben H. Fleet Science Center).

continued on page 85

Boy Scouts perform a variety of tasks in front of the Indian Village. After the first exposition the village became Boy Scout Headquarters, 1935. *San Diego Historical Society*

DUCK POND AT BALBOA PARK, C. 1927 *San Diego Historical Society*

THE FINE ARTS GALLERY (LATER THE SAN DIEGO MUSEUM OF ART) WAS DESIGNED BY WILLIAM TEMPLETON JOHNSON AND OPENED IN 1926.
APPLETON AND AMELIA BRIDGES PROVIDED MOST OF THE $400,000 IN FUNDING. *San Diego Historical Society*

Entrance of the Civic Auditorium, formerly the Southern Counties Building — the auditorium opened in 1920 and was used for concerts, theater and other functions until it burned down in 1925, hours before the annual Fireman's Ball, c. 1920. *San Diego Historical Society*

Power plays

In the 1920s San Diego was prosperous enough to engage in a healthy political fight over its beloved Balboa Park. In 1925 the zoo board sought a City Charter amendment that would have given the board full control over its 123 acres, and no longer be required to answer to the Board of Park Commissioners. "The Zoological Society is non-political and always will be," Harry Wegeforth told a Women's Civic Center audience. "A park board is appointed by the mayor, usually in discharge of political debts, and of necessity is in politics. Keep the zoo out of politics by vesting its control in the public-spirited organization which has created it."

George Marston warned that a future zoo board, unfettered by park policies, "might do great injury to the park and stir up any amount of trouble." It would be wiser, he said, for the park board to continue to exert full control over land use in the park.

In a statement quoted ever after down through the decades, Marston wrote in the *Union*: "Balboa Park is primarily a park, to be cherished as a place of natural beauty. Although it is one of the largest parks in the country, the time is coming when the building of hospitals and school houses, or even libraries and museums, must cease, or else we shall have a city there instead of a park." The proposed amendment was defeated, 3,847 in favor, 6,088 opposed. However, in November 1934, the voters did approve a

special property tax for zoo maintenance. The income from this source for fiscal year 2000 was projected at about $4.1 million, less than 5 percent of the Zoological Society's $120 million operating and capital budget.

The other major fight in this period concerned a proposal to build a new home for San Diego State Teachers College. Its 1,500 students had outgrown their State Normal School site at El Cajon and Park boulevards, and a mayor's committee recommended granting 125 acres in the northeast corner of Balboa Park. Supporters said the college would complement the primarily weekend park use by families, museumgoers and zoo visitors. "Don't confine its usefulness to Saturday and Sunday, make it work 365 days a year for youth and for ambitious manhood and womanhood," said attorney Leland G. Stanford.

But park defenders argued otherwise. "The people who ask the great mass of common people to give away their recreation ground say you don't need this great breathing space as all you have to do is to get into your automobiles and go to the backcountry," said architect Lincoln Rogers. "What about the 50 to 60 percent of the common people that have no automobiles?" Voters agreed with Rogers, Marston and others and turned down the proposal 6,561 in favor, 15,560 opposed.

THE FLEET OF TAXIS BELONGING TO THE YELLOW CAB CO. ALONG PARK BOULEVARD NEAR THE INDIAN VILLAGE, c. 1928
San Diego Historical Society

FINE ARTS GALLERY (SAN DIEGO MUSEUM OF ART) OPENS.

1926

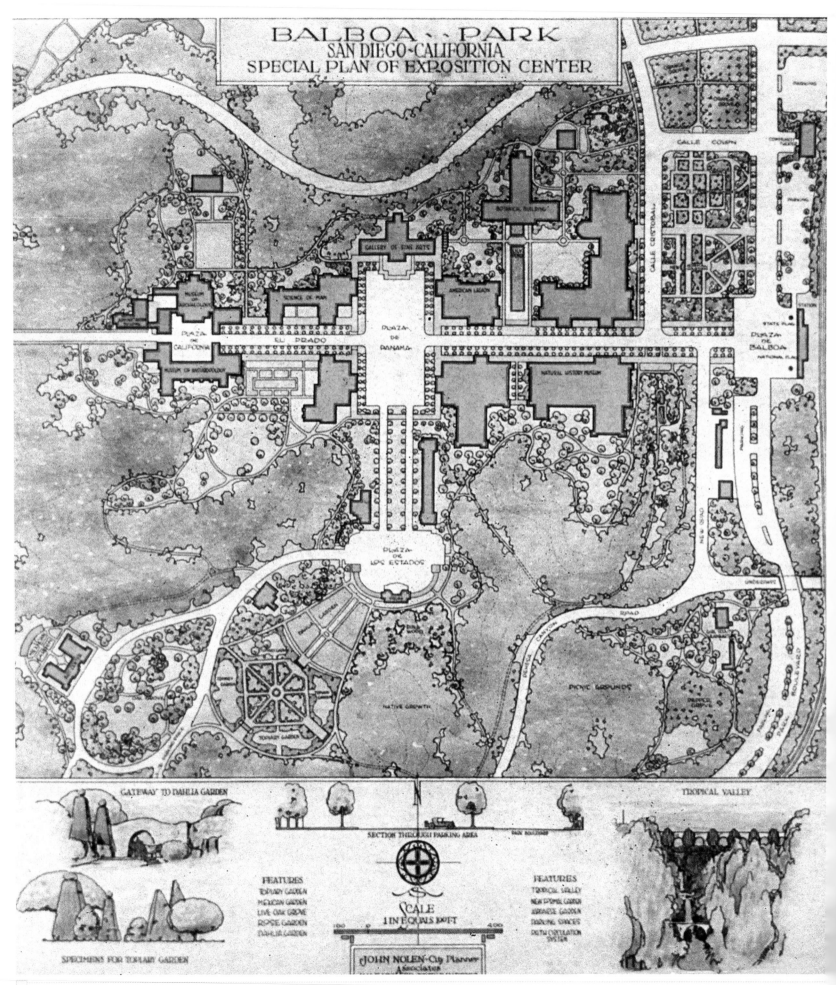

BALBOA · PARK
SAN DIEGO · CALIFORNIA
SPECIAL PLAN OF EXPOSITION CENTER

JOHN NOLEN'S 1927 PARK PLAN INCORPORATED EXPOSITION BUILDINGS AND, TO THE EAST OF FLORIDA CANYON, PROPOSED WHAT LATER BECAME THE MORLEY FIELD RECREATION AREA.

Architectural Archives, University of Pennsylvania

AERIAL VIEW OF THE NEARLY COMPLETED NAVAL HOSPITAL, C. 1921 *San Diego Historical Society*

In 1928 they approved a new location at Montezuma Mesa for what is now San Diego State University. One wonders how the park and university would have coexisted as enrollment grew to 30,000 two generations later.

In 1925 Marston underwrote another comprehensive city planning effort by John Nolen, and the park board added the additional assignment to write a new plan for Balboa Park. The 1905 effort by Samuel Parsons Jr. had been severely compromised by the 1915-16 exposition and other developments.

In addition to bemoaning the nonpark encroachments by schools and the Naval Hospital, Nolen regretted that many trees had obscured the spectacular views to the mountains and ocean that Parsons had so admired. "In many cases, existing trees already planted in the park should be cut out to open up views and also to give the best trees nearby a chance to grow," he said in his February 1927 report.

Nolen's most important recommendation was to turn the rejected college campus site into a recreation center. "A large athletic field and parade ground is strongly recommended for early development in the northeast corner of the park. Here practically every type of recreation could be provided." With $300,000 in bonds and Depression-era federal funds, this proposal was implemented and Morley Field's sporting facilities follow closely what Nolen proposed.

A paradise at last

Ten years after the 1915-16 exposition, Balboa Park had truly become a cultural and recreational mecca. In addition to the zoo, Spreckels Organ Pavilion and museums, the San Diego Players community theater company performed in the Yorick Theater. (This was the exposition's U.S. Fisheries Building, razed in the 1930s to make way for Spanish Village). The American Legion converted the Home Economy Building into a war memorial with a library and offices for patriotic organizations. (The Timken Museum of Art today occupies that building site.) The San Diego Floral Association organized flower shows southwest of the organ pavilion. Nearby was an art center and school, directed by Kanuela Searle.

Recreational facilities included the 18-hole golf course on the East Mesa, Golden Hill Park and playground, shuffleboard and roque courts on Sixth Avenue and tennis courts south of the Boy Scout camp. Balboa Stadium, built for the exposition, served both San Diego High School and the city at large. (President Wilson spoke there in 1919 to promote the League of Nations.) "Here, indeed, is a paradise where one may wander by the hour," the 1925 *Balboa Park Souvenir Guide* said, "finding at every turn beauty in its most exalted forms." In 1929, the park was nominated as one of the world's 10 best examples of landscape architecture.

continued on page 94

COSTUMED PATRONS IN FRONT OF THE BALBOA PARK RIDING ACADEMY, 1932 *San Diego Historical Society*

"El Cid," San Diego's first outdoor public sculpture was unveiled in 1930. The sculptor, Anna Hyatt Huntington, and her husband, who founded the Hispanic Society in America, donated the statue of the medieval Spanish hero. *San Diego Historical Society*

HUMPHREY J. STEWART (1854-1932), SPRECKELS ORGAN PAVILION ORGANIST, 1932 — HE PLAYED DAILY ORGAN CONCERTS DURING THE 1915
EXPOSITION AND CONTINUED TO PERFORM UNTIL 1932. *San Diego Historical Society*

CABRILLO BRIDGE BECAME MERELY AN EXTENSION TO LAUREL STREET IN THE 1920S FOR MOTORISTS SEEKING A SHORTCUT BETWEEN THE EAST AND WEST SIDES OF BALBOA PARK. *San Diego Historical Society*

Commerce as well as culture thrived in the park. San Diegans were buying houses in new suburbs spreading out along streetcar lines. And so, it made sense to launch a "Better Homes" exposition there in May 1927. Builders advertised their new housing subdivisions, many featuring bungalows in the highly popular Spanish Colonial or Mission Revival style. The Realtors Glee Club entertained home buyers and the Chamber of Commerce put on a skit, "Good Business." The first prize for most original and unique booth went to the Quality Building and Securities Company for a miniature plastic stucco dwelling.

Balboa Park had one more shining moment before the park's future became clouded with the onset of the Depression. On July 5, 1930, Alejandro Padilla y Bell, Spanish

ambassador to the United States, unveiled a statue in the Plaza de Panama of Rodrigo Díaz, the medieval Spanish hero known as El Cid who battled the Moors in the 11th century. Sculpted by Anna Hyatt Huntington, the 23-foot, six-ton bronze man on horseback was San Diego's first piece of outdoor public sculpture. Mrs. Huntington's husband, Archer, had founded the Hispanic Society of America in New York (location of the original of this sculpture). The Huntingtons were friends of Fine Arts Gallery architect William Templeton Johnson and offered to donate an art library as well as the statue.

Just five days after the statue's dedication, a front-page story in the *Union* carried the news that the Fine Arts

ROYAL A. BROWN (1890-1954), SPRECKELS ORGAN PAVILION ORGANIST, PERFORMED INTO THE 1950S, SUCCEEDING THE FIRST CIVIC ORGANIST, HUMPHREY J. STEWART, c. 1928. *San Diego Historical Society*

Gallery, San Diego Museum and Natural History Museum would have to close because of threatened budget cuts. "Nothing tends to aggravate hard times so much as the extravagant timidity which leads businessmen and public officials to curtail essential activities at the moment when depression appears," the newspaper editorialized. "The attendance records, the national publicity, the opinions of our leading citizens, all go to prove beyond any doubt that the institutions in question here are among San Diego's essential assets. To impair them is to serve notice to every citizen and to untold thousands of visitors that San Diego is in desperate circumstances." A few days later, some of the cuts were rescinded and the museums were not closed. "We can get by on a skimpy basis," Park Commissioner Marston said.

Raze or restore

In 1932 as San Diego and the rest of the nation settled into the Depression, the future of Balboa Park looked bleak. With tax receipts falling, the City Council wielded a sharp budget ax that spared few departments. In a celebrated stunt, county assessor James H. Johnson held an auction of zoo animals, claiming the zoo was in default of $6,354 in personal property taxes. "I don't think I need a zoo," said one onlooker, who declined to make a bid. Humphrey J. Stewart, 78, civic organist since 1915, quit after his salary for daily concerts at the Spreckels Organ Pavilion was slashed.

Stewart gave his last concert August 31 and died less than four months later.

Most serious were the rapidly deteriorating conditions of the exposition buildings and grounds. After the head of a palm tree fell to the ground, killing a two-year-old girl in 1933, inspectors found widespread evidence of termite damage. City inspector Oscar G. Knecht estimated the cost of rehabilitation in March 1933 at $256,200, more than the cost of the just completed Natural History Museum building. Knecht recommended against the improvements, even if the funds were available. "The buildings have no practical value other than to grace the vision of visitors," he said, warning that a strong earthquake such as one that had just hit Long Beach March 10 could level what he termed "junk buildings." City electrician A.E. Johnstone noted that the 1915 exposition buildings had all been exempted from city electrical code standards and were "very dangerous to life and property." The Park Board agreed with the inspectors and recommended razing all the temporary buildings and replacing them with landscaping. "Lawns, flowers, artistic fountains and perhaps a romantic colonnade on each side of the driveway [El Prado] would be more beautiful and attractive than the present setup," the board said in a statement. "Many of our finest parks consist principally of the beauties of nature."

The reaction from the public was swift and resourceful. Gertrude Gilbert, who had headed the musical programs at the Panama-California Exposition,

continued on page 100

THE NATURAL HISTORY MUSEUM JUST PRIOR TO COMPLETION, C. 1933 — CONSTRUCTION ON A NORTH WING WAS DELAYED UNTIL 1998. *San Diego Historical Society*

1933

Construction in the palisades area southwest of the Organ Pavilion for the 1935-36 California Pacific International Exposition *San Diego Historical Society*

California Pa

Color drawing of the lily pond and the House of Hospitality by Frank E. Brown for a pictorial booklet
illustrating highlights of the exposition, 1935 *San Diego Historical Society*

c International Exposition
PICTORIAL

San Diego, California
1 9 3 5-6

FRANK E. BRO

appealed to San Diego's pride in having a park filled with buildings unequaled elsewhere. "The people of San Diego should consider seriously what the loss of the park buildings will mean to the city before they allow these architectural gems to be destroyed and the city deprived of its one real asset of physical beauty," Gilbert said. "Once they are down, they can never be replaced, but as long as they remain standing, even in a state of temporary preservation, there is always a chance of their permanent rehabilitation... We must make a desperate effort to retain these buildings, which have become so dear to the hearts of our own citizens."

She marched off to the male-dominated Chamber of Commerce and got its president, David N. Millan, to appoint a committee to investigate the buildings and prepare an independent assessment of the repairs necessary. In a week, local architect Richard Requa and contractor Walter Trepte estimated the cost at $70,000, just $2,000 more than demolishing and landscaping would have cost. The City Council responded with a 30-day reprieve to see if the funds could be raised. By the time the work commenced, local residents and businesses had contributed $77,000 in materials and federal and state relief programs pitched in $300,000 worth of labor costs. This campaign lengthened some of the temporary buildings' lifespan for an additional 60 years.

Drugan's dream

The Long Beach quake that awakened San Diegans to the need to save or raze their exposition buildings also changed the life of Frank Drugan. A former field representative of the Scripps-Howard newspaper chain, Drugan lost his home and office in the quake and moved to San Diego in August 1933. He saw the park buildings and began a quiet campaign to host another exposition in them once they were restored. The next month he visited the Century of Progress fair in Chicago and inquired about moving some of the exhibits to San Diego after that fair's scheduled closing in 1934. From Chicago he continued to New York in November to win support of the Scripps-Howard officials. In Washington he looked into securing federal-relief support.

Back in San Diego by Thanksgiving, he moved into a small office on the top floor of the U.S. Grant Hotel and began talking up the fair. By March 1934 he presented his proposal to the Chamber of

EXPOSITION VISITORS STROLLING ALONG THE PLAZA DE AMERICA IN FRONT OF THE CALIFORNIA STATE BUILDING, 1935; THE GARDENS WERE REMOVED AFTER THE FAIR TO MAKE WAY FOR A PARKING LOT. *San Diego Historical Society*

Commerce and by April the campaign was on to raise $300,000 for an initial budget. The California Pacific International Exposition was incorporated in July and the final funding totaling $700,000 was obtained Sept. 19. The *Union* hailed Drugan as a "human dynamo" for getting the new fair rolling. Said G. Aubrey Davidson, the 1915 fair veteran and chairman of the 1935 fair, "As a result of the exposition, San Diego will be the most talked of city in the United States. It is truly remarkable that in times like these a community united in purpose and determined to work its way forward can put together an undertaking of this kind."

With Richard Requa as consulting architect and Zack Farmer as managing director (he oversaw the 1932 Los Angeles Olympic Games), the exposition board hired 211 staff members, including a Hollywood set designer, Juan Larrinaga. Up to 2,700 construction workers restored and adapted the old exposition buildings and constructed a set of new ones in the Palisades area southwest of the Spreckels Organ Pavilion. The final cost: $1.23 million. The old buildings and streets were renamed and many of the new buildings were designed to reflect architecture before and after the Spanish Colonial period. Among the most noteworthy additions were the Ford Building, constructed by the car company to showcase transportation; the Ford (now Starlight) Bowl amphitheater; 15 cottages comprising the House of Pacific Relations; Spanish Village, laid out like a quaint Mexican village; and the Old Globe Theatre behind the California Quadrangle.

The most notable new landscaping feature built for the fair was Del Rey Moro Garden behind the House of Hospitality. Requa patterned it after the garden at the Casa del Rey Moro in Ronda, Spain. He also redesigned the Montezuma Garden into the Alcazar Garden;

continued on page 113

RICHARD REQUA (1881-1941), CONSULTING ARCHITECT FOR THE CALIFORNIA PACIFIC INTERNATIONAL EXPOSITION, REMODELED SEVERAL OF THE FIRST EXPOSITION BUILDINGS, INCLUDING THE HOUSE OF HOSPITALITY, AND ESTABLISHED THE VARYING STYLES IN THE PALISADES AREA FOR NEW EXPO BUILDINGS. HE WAS INSTRUMENTAL IN POPULARIZING THE MISSION REVIVAL STYLE OF ARCHITECTURE FOR MANY SAN DIEGO NEIGHBORHOODS.
San Diego Historical Society

4434 STANDARD OIL TOWER AND FORD EXPOSITION BUILDING

AMERICA'S EXPOSITION, SAN DIEGO, CALIFORNIA

THE STANDARD OIL TOWER AND THE FORD BUILDING DURING THE EXPOSITION, 1935

San Diego Historical Society

THE OLD GLOBE THEATER BEGAN PRESENTING PLAYS DURING THE EXPOSITION, 1935. AFTER THE EXPOSITION A ROOF WAS ADDED AND PRODUCTIONS BECAME A PERMANENT FIXTURE IN THE PARK.

San Diego Historical Society

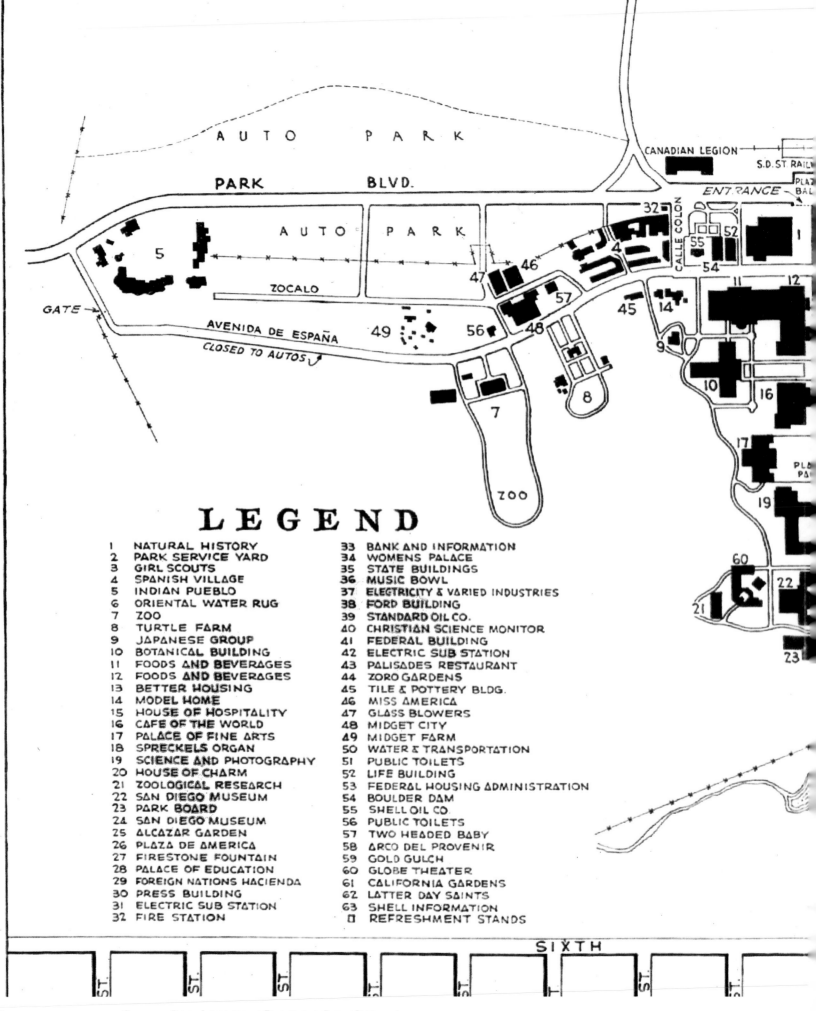

AUTO PARK

CANADIAN LEGION

S.D. ST RAILW

PARK BLVD.

AUTO PARK

ENTRANCE - BAL

32

CALLE COLON

55 52

4 54

5

ZOCALO

47 46

45 14

57

GATE

AVENIDA DE ESPAÑA

49 56 48

9

CLOSED TO AUTOS

11 12

7

8

10 16

17

ZOO

19

60

21 22

23

LEGEND

1	NATURAL HISTORY	33	BANK AND INFORMATION
2	PARK SERVICE YARD	34	WOMENS PALACE
3	GIRL SCOUTS	35	STATE BUILDINGS
4	SPANISH VILLAGE	36	MUSIC BOWL
5	INDIAN PUEBLO	37	ELECTRICITY & VARIED INDUSTRIES
6	ORIENTAL WATER RUG	38	FORD BUILDING
7	ZOO	39	STANDARD OIL CO.
8	TURTLE FARM	40	CHRISTIAN SCIENCE MONITOR
9	JAPANESE GROUP	41	FEDERAL BUILDING
10	BOTANICAL BUILDING	42	ELECTRIC SUB STATION
11	FOODS AND BEVERAGES	43	PALISADES RESTAURANT
12	FOODS AND BEVERAGES	44	ZORO GARDENS
13	BETTER HOUSING	45	TILE & POTTERY BLDG.
14	MODEL HOME	46	MISS AMERICA
15	HOUSE OF HOSPITALITY	47	GLASS BLOWERS
16	CAFE OF THE WORLD	48	MIDGET CITY
17	PALACE OF FINE ARTS	49	MIDGET FARM
18	SPRECKELS ORGAN	50	WATER & TRANSPORTATION
19	SCIENCE AND PHOTOGRAPHY	51	PUBLIC TOILETS
20	HOUSE OF CHARM	52	LIFE BUILDING
21	ZOOLOGICAL RESEARCH	53	FEDERAL HOUSING ADMINISTRATION
22	SAN DIEGO MUSEUM	54	BOULDER DAM
23	PARK BOARD	55	SHELL OIL CO.
24	SAN DIEGO MUSEUM	56	PUBLIC TOILETS
25	ALCAZAR GARDEN	57	TWO HEADED BABY
26	PLAZA DE AMERICA	58	ARCO DEL PROVENIR
27	FIRESTONE FOUNTAIN	59	GOLD GULCH
28	PALACE OF EDUCATION	60	GLOBE THEATER
29	FOREIGN NATIONS HACIENDA	61	CALIFORNIA GARDENS
30	PRESS BUILDING	62	LATTER DAY SAINTS
31	ELECTRIC SUB STATION	63	SHELL INFORMATION
32	FIRE STATION	☐	REFRESHMENT STANDS

SIXTH

ST. ST. ST. ST. ST. ST. ST. ST.

GENERAL GROUND PLAN OF THE CALIFORNIA PACIFIC INTERNATIONAL EXPOSITION IN BALBOA PARK, 1936
San Diego Historical Society

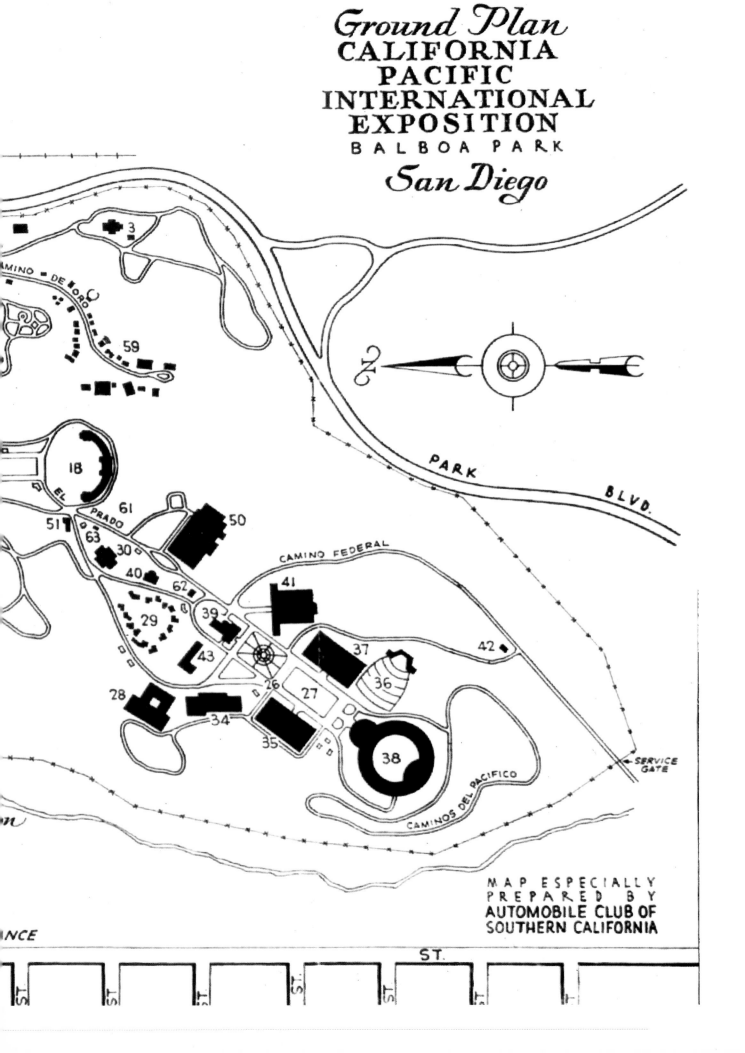

Ground Plan
CALIFORNIA
PACIFIC
INTERNATIONAL
EXPOSITION
BALBOA PARK
San Diego

The Gold Gulch "Days of 49" mining camp exhibit allowed exposition visitors the opportunity to experience California's 1849 gold rush, 1935. *San Diego Historical Society*

ROBOT KIDNAPS QUEEN ZORINE OF THE NUDIST COLONY IN ZORO GARDENS, 1935 *San Diego Historical Society*

Drink Coca-Cola
THE PAUSE THAT REFRESHES

EMPLOYEES AT A FOOD AND BEVERAGE STAND, 1935 *San Diego Historical Society*

A CHOIR AND BAND GIVING A CONCERT AT THE FORD BOWL (LATER THE STARLIGHT BOWL) DURING THE EXPOSITION, 1935 *San Diego Historical Society*

MECHANICAL MAN WITH GUN AND PROFESSOR HARRY MAY, 1935 *San Diego Historical Society*

opened up the interior of the House of Hospitality building to include a patio with a tiled fountain and sculpture ("La Tehuana") by San Diego artist Donal Hord; and inserted a tiled fountain resembling a Persian carpet into the quiet breezeway east of the House of Hospitality. To highlight the buildings and landscaping in a new way, H.O. Davis and his electricians installed flood lights and colored lights that made the fair a visual sensation by night.

Crowd pleasers

Besides buildings, fairgoers liked the Firestone fountain and Standard Oil of California's 108-foot "Tower to the Sun" in the newly created Plaza de America; the "Arco del Futuro" and reflecting pools in the Plaza de Panama; Gold Gulch, an ersatz '49ers mining town in the canyon now occupied by the Japanese Friendship Garden; Modeltown, 120 scale-model homes designed by prominent architects for the Federal Housing Administration; and perhaps the most unusual of all, the nudist colony at the Zoro Gardens grotto at the east end of the Prado. "Zorine" and her band celebrated the clotheless lifestyle as a healthy alternative and authorities generally tolerated this display of nonconformity behind a wooden fence (with strategically placed knotholes for peeping fairgoers).

At the fun zone located on the site of the 1915 Isthmus and this time called the Midway, more than 100 midgets worked and played in their own "city." Ripley's Believe-It-Or-Not presented a "four-legged" girl. And American Indians returned to the 1915 village. The San Diego Zoo, Natural History Museum, Fine Arts Gallery and San Diego Museum continued in operation with added attractions. For example, the art gallery, dubbed the Palace of Fine Arts, had drawings by Walt Disney on display. Major symphony orchestras performed nightly at Ford Bowl.

Visitors included President Franklin D. Roosevelt, who had visited the first exposition as assistant secretary of the Navy, former President Herbert Hoover, boxer Jack Dempsey and evangelist Amee Semple McPherson. When sexy film star Mae West arrived June 9, 1935, she quipped, "I'm sorry I didn't know the fleet was coming in tomorrow as I certainly would have come down then. I'm very patriotic that way."

The fair extended

As with the first exposition, the success of drawing nearly 4.8 million visitors to San Diego convinced officials to extend the 1935 fair for a second year. The Midway was replaced by an Amusement Zone. Instead of Midget Village there was to be a "Mickey Mouse Circus" starring Leo Singer's midgets (some of whom later appeared in the 1939 movie *Wizard of Oz*). Enchanted Land featured Mother Goose and fairy tale figures. Indian Village was reoccupied by the

Boy Scouts and Gold Gulch closed down. *Zoro* nudists remained, sans Zorine. One new entertainment act was Sally Rand, the bubble dancer. The exhibition buildings also contained new items and works of art. On opening day, February 12, 1936, press reports promised visitors would find "an entire new exposition."

Although only 2 million visited during the second season, by the time it closed on California Admission Day, September 9, 1936, most San Diegans considered Balboa Park and its buildings and grounds a gem to be preserved and treasured. One young visitor, Elaine Steele, filled three scrapbooks with headlines, souvenirs (including a crushed popcorn box) and dozens of clippings. She noted every visit (52 in two years) and whom she accompanied.

San Diego had shown again it could entertain the world. In the depths of the Depression, a 25-cent admission offered an escape to a wonderland made possible because a few citizens refused to let the old buildings die, and a newcomer promoted the fair tirelessly until the business community got on board.

Old questions returned

Yet, when the hawkers stopped hawking and Sally Rand stopped dancing, the old questions of the park and its purpose resurfaced. Should it be for recreation or education, quiet enjoyment or cultural enrichment? Banker Joseph W. Sefton Jr. was opposed to leaving the second exposition buildings in place. "They are hideous and badly placed," he argued. "Had we torn out the 1915 exposition buildings and landscaped the park we would have a beautiful place there now and not a long row of ramshackle firetraps ... One of these days a fire will sweep them all out anyhow." Nevertheless San Diegans wanted the buildings to stay.

A month after the exposition closed, Julius Wangenheim, chairman of the Park Rehabilitation Committee appointed by City Manager R.W. Flack, recommended which buildings to retain and how to use them. The committee also recommended returning to the "very romantic names" used in 1915; thus, the Plaza del Pacifico became the Plaza de Panama and the Avenida de Palacios, El Prado.

New ideas for new park uses appeared. The Ford Building would become a planetarium. Radio Station KGB would lease 100 acres for a transmitter tower. A Cabrillo festival in 1942 would mark the 400th anniversary of Cabrillo's discovery of San Diego. City Councilman Fred Simpson dusted off the old idea of selling part of the park in order to pay for construction of a series of neighborhood parks. Banker Frank Belcher backed a permanent San Diego Trade Exposition in the park. The Mission Indian Federation proposed a permanent national Indian museum controlled and operated by Indians. In July 1937 a business group at the U.S. Grant Hotel heard plans for a $1 million convention center in the park northeast of

continued on page 118

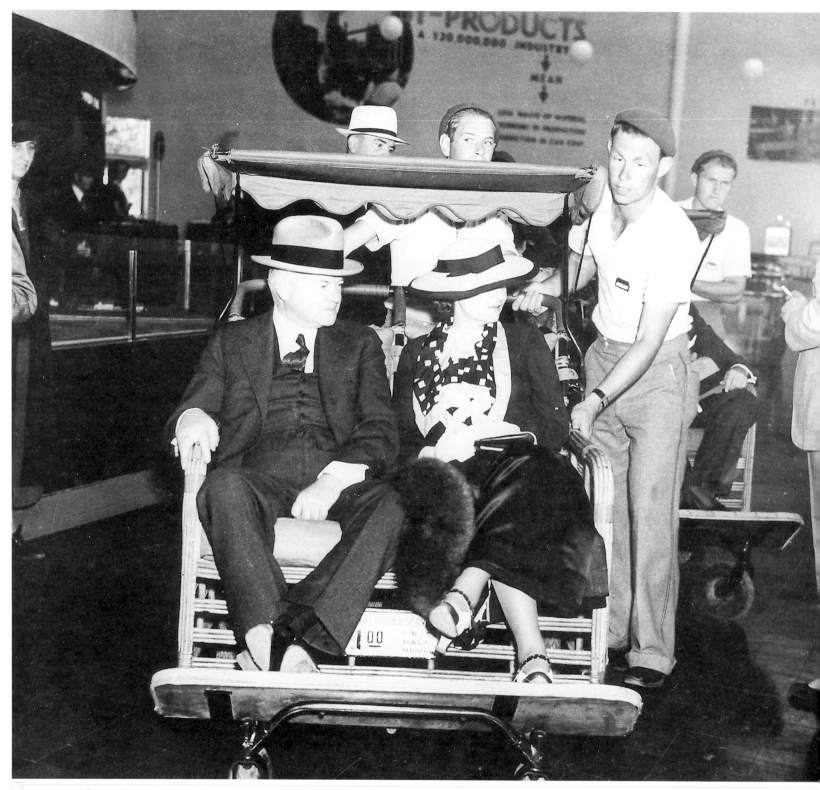

FORMER PRESIDENT HERBERT HOOVER WAS ESCORTED THROUGH ONE OF THE EXHIBITION HALLS DURING THE OPENING OF THE EXPOSITION, 1935. *San Diego Historical Society*

Luncheon for First Lady Eleanor Roosevelt at the House of Hospitality during the exposition, 1935 *San Diego Historical Society*

A couple enjoying tea-time at the Midget Village, 1935 *San Diego Historical Society*

SALLY RAND, FAN DANCER, AT THE EXPOSITION, 1936 *San Diego Historical Society*

W. Allen Perry
(1903-1999),
Landscape architect at
the California Pacific
International Exposition,
was named park superin-
tendent in 1939. He
nearly lost his job when
he objected to building a
freeway through Balboa
Park. He later pursued a
successful banking
career as marketing
director for San Diego
Trust & Savings Bank.
San Diego Historical Society

Spanish Village. "About $4 billion will be spent in holding conventions in this country next year," said one speaker. "We could bring our share of that money to San Diego if we had hall facilities."

One idea that did survive was the decision to retain the Old Globe Theatre as a permanent playhouse. The open-air seating area was enclosed and the San Diego Community Theatre began producing plays there in 1937. One young actor who was to figure prominently in the Globe's destiny for more than 60 years was Craig Noel.

The park had been designed originally as a retreat from the city, where families could play and picnic. But the advent of the automobile impacted the park as well as the rest of San Diego. The Prado became a motorized extension of Laurel Street, a shortcut from Hillcrest to North Park. Despite opposition from the now-advisory Park and Recreation Commission, the City Council and voters approved construction of the city's first freeway through Cabrillo Canyon beneath Cabrillo Bridge. In 1939, acting City Manager Fred Rhodes attempted to fire Park Director W. Allen Perry, who disagreed with the park freeway plan.

War intervenes

Another exposition, a big convention center and radio towers — none of these went anywhere when the Japanese attacked Pearl Harbor, Hawaii, on December 7, 1941. The park donned a military uniform and went to war for the second time in 24 years. California National Guard General R.E. Mittelstadt ordered 1,000 Army men to occupy buildings in the park. But three days later, Navy Captain Byron McCandless, acting commandant of the 11th Naval District, informed City Manager W.W. Cooper that the Balboa Naval Hospital would need eight park buildings immediately and four others soon thereafter; the Army moved to other quarters in the city. The City Council revoked all park use and occupancy permits by month's end (with the exception of the zoo and three park museums). "Now we know a little how it feels to be a refugee," said the women at the House of Hospitality, whose organizational tenants had to vacate their spaces to make way for nurses who would live in the building for the next four years.

The park museums continued in business for more than a year, but by March 1943, they, too, closed their doors. The Fine Arts Gallery relocated some of its works to a private home in Mission Hills and sent other paintings out of state. The Museum of Man (renamed as such in 1942) shipped some items to other museums and stored others; its staff retained offices on the second floor. The Natural History Museum encased its dinosaur exhibits and other large items while also retaining some office space. In all, the three museums made room for 2,142 hospital beds. The Navy covered the costs of moving, storage and staff.

The Old Globe Theatre complex was transformed into a movie theater, classroom, church, barber shop and scullery. The Japanese Tea Garden became a Red Cross Servicemen's club. Spanish Village and the Indian Village hosted the 204th Army Anti-Aircraft Artillery Unit. At the zoo, early concerns about animals loosened during expected Japanese bombing raids soon receded. Royal A. Brown lost his job as city organist when it became too difficult for the public to get to the organ pavilion. The Morley Field swimming pool remained in public use and the Botanical Building's Lily Pond was deepened so it could be used for swimming and boating instruction and as a convalescent pool.

Renamed "Camp Kidd" in honor of Rear Admiral Isaac C. Kidd, who died at Pearl Harbor, the Palisades area of Balboa Park was at first an extension of the Naval Training Center and then a hospital corpsman school. The Ford Building was not occupied by the Navy but by a Consolidated Aircraft Corporation (later General Dynamics/Convair) vocational school. The Spreckels Organ Pavilion became a dispensary, dental clinic and "patients theater." The city permitted the Navy to build temporary buildings in Pan-American Plaza and behind the Federal Building on condition they be removed within six months of the military's departure. All these arrangements were made by means of memos and letters. The city could not formally lease the park and its buildings to the military because the City Charter required a public vote for that purpose.

Balboa Park made an ideal setting for the 12,000 men and women who worked or recuperated at the expanded Balboa Naval Hospital. "All hours of the day," wrote park director W. Allen Perry in *California Garden* magazine in the fall of 1944, "you will find these men with their shirts off, or in trunks, taking up the actinic [radiating] rays as eagerly as any shrub or flower. Others are out in their wheelchairs. Perhaps the happiest are those which are wheeled right out on their beds. With their blankets off and the legs of their pajamas rolled up, these men are getting one of the most important medications of all. And the colors of the flowers are temporarily of little significance compared with the deepening, glowing suntans of these fighting men."

Park unknown

Two fairs and two wars: It had been quite a growing-up period for Balboa Park. At war's end, there were so many new residents of San Diego that many had never had full access to the park in peacetime. As the *Union* wrote in September 1945:

"San Diego's 1,400-acre Balboa Park is pretty much a mystery to thousands of the city's new residents who have made their homes here since the war… Only prewar residents can recall the summer open-air concerts in the Ford [Starlight] Bowl, leisurely

NAVY NURSES POSING IN THE GARDEN OF THE CAFÉ DEL REY MORO WHICH WAS USED AS A MESS HALL, C. 1943.
San Diego Historical Society

walks through the botanical garden, the organ recitals by noted musicians on the Spreckels outdoor organ, afternoons at the San Diego Fine Arts Gallery, hours spent studying the relics of older civilizations housed in the museum of archaeology and anthropology — better known as the Museum of Man — or days of study and relaxation in the Natural History Museum."

It was now time for San Diego, oldtimers and newcomers, to take back the park and prepare it for the second half of the 20th century. The task reopened longstanding debates about the park's role and function. Officials promised to restore and improve the park, but it would take decades and tens of millions of dollars to complete the task.

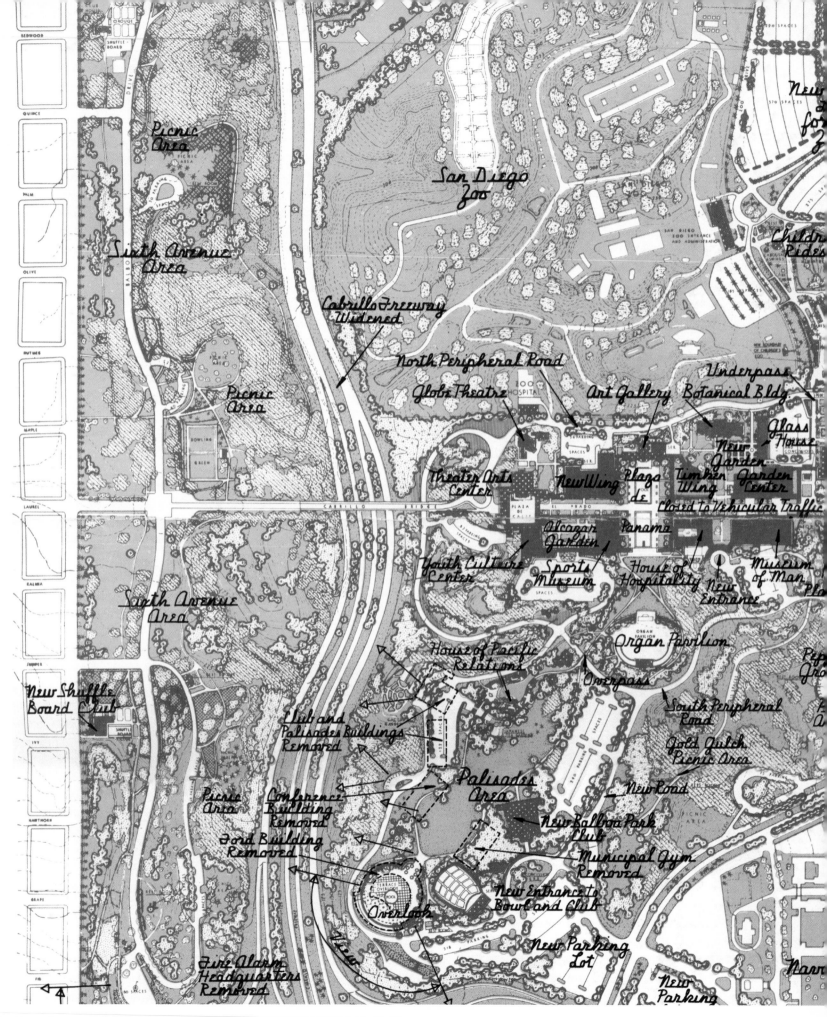

MASTER PLAN FOR BALBOA PARK, SAN DIEGO, CALIFORNIA, 1960

San Diego Historical Society

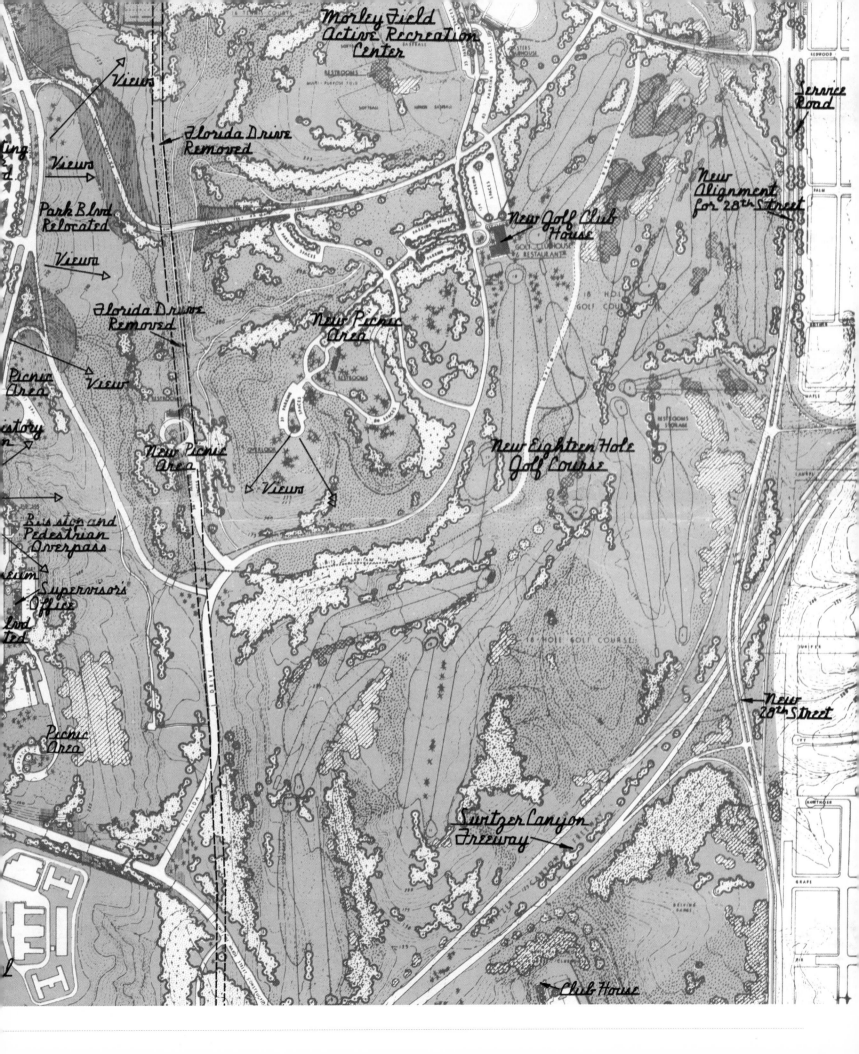

Morley Field
Active Recreation
Center

Views

Florida Drive
Removed

Views

Park Blvd.
Relocated

Views

Florida Drive
Removed

View

Picnic
Area

New Picnic
Area

istory

New Picnic
Area

Views

Bus stop and
Pedestrian
Overpass

eum

Supervisor's
Office

lvd.
ted

Picnic
Area

New
Alignment
for 28th Street

Service
Road

New Golf Club
House

New Picnic
Area

New Eighteen Hole
Golf Course

New
28th Street

Switzer Canyon
Freeway

Club House

A Park
Unfinished
1945 — The Present

Chapter Three

"*San Diego is a city with a park for a heart… Balboa Park is not finished. Neither is San Diego.*"

— *Lew Scarr, The San Diego Union, 1969*

Within a month of the Japanese surrender on August 14, 1945, the Navy began its plans to surrender Balboa Park back to San Diego. "The buildings here are in no way suited for permanent hospital use," said Captain John Ruddock, the Balboa Naval Hospital's chief of medicine. "We do not want huge halls for wards or buildings scattered as they are here. We are grateful to the people of San Diego for letting us have it when we needed it, but we shall also be glad when permanent facilities can take care of the need."

The park's greatest defender did not live to see the postwar vision unfold. George W. Marston died quietly at age 95 on May 31, 1946. In his eulogy, James A. Blaisdell noted Marston's connection to the park: "Just around the corner lies the central Balboa Park of the city — walks that he laid out — flowers that he planted — trees that he loved — vistas that he foresaw — beautiful buildings that he envisioned. Down these walks he passed meditatively at evening or early morning. This paradise was not here when George Marston came [in 1870]. In this park he speaks to thousands whose lives have been made happier through him."

Oversight of the park's future passed to a special committee chaired by another longtime park defender, G. Aubrey Davidson, the man who proposed the first exposition and helped lead the second. Officially, the city regained possession of the park October 1, 1946, but major repairs could not start without money. The federal government delivered a $790,000 check in February 1947 to cover the daunting task of clearing away temporary buildings, removing partitions within buildings and making the buildings and grounds hospitable to the public. At first, there were great hopes that the park would spring back to life as the museums reopened and new attractions were planned.

• The 1915 Indian Village was razed in July 1946 after it was declared a fire hazard and then replaced four years later by the Veterans War Memorial Building.

• New chimes in the California Tower, donated by Frank Lowe in honor of his mother, Ona May Lowe, were played for the first time on Christmas Day, 1946 — the first public program in the park in five years.

• A new Municipal Gym opened a month later in the former Palace of Electricity and Varied Industries.

• Starlight Opera produced musicals in the zoo's Wegeforth Bowl, starting in July 1946, and two years later moved to Balboa Park (no longer "Ford") Bowl.

• The Spreckels Organ Pavilion began offering free public concerts again in April 1947 (and got a $5,420 facelift in 1949).

• The Boy Scouts dedicated a new camp in May 1948.

• The Old Globe opened its first postwar season in October

AERIAL VIEW OF BALBOA PARK ON CHRISTMAS EVE, 1953 *San Diego Historical Society*

AFTER BEING DECLARED A FIRE HAZARD, INDIAN VILLAGE WAS BURNED DOWN IN 1946. IT WAS REPLACED BY THE VETERANS WAR MEMORIAL BUILDING.
San Diego Historical Society

1948 with William Saroyan's "Time of Your Life" and launched a summer Shakespeare Festival in 1949.

Most of the groups that occupied park buildings before the war got their use permits back, though there were some minor disagreements about lease terms. For example, the Spanish Village artists group balked at the monthly rents they were expected to pay — 10 cents per square foot, four times what the artists said they could afford. The House of Pacific Relations international cottages wanted free rent; the city manager recommended a $5 monthly fee for each building.

As usual, it was time again to patch up or pull down the aging "temporary" 1915-16 exposition buildings that had weathered two wars and a second fair. In April 1947, 77-year-old Frederick Law Olmsted Jr., who with his cousin had quit in 1911 as planners of the first exposition, advised the city to remove four or five of the buildings and to replace them with gardens until new permanent buildings could be erected in some places. "The geometrically increasing cost per annum of keeping in repair such flimsily built plaster representations of masonry architecture," Olmsted said, "makes it imperative to decide promptly (a) just which of these much admired structures are now to be completely reconstructed of durable materials as permanent features of the park and (b) what is now to be done with the rest of them."

The city's chief building inspector, Oscar Knecht, who had condemned the same buildings in 1933, followed up on Olmsted's advice and declared seven buildings structurally unfit. Fire Marshal Al Penrose agreed. Lovers of the exposition buildings countered that they should be repaired, not razed. "The Navy has just paid to San Diego more than $800,000 [sic] to make good any damage done to these buildings and adjacent grounds," said G. Aubrey Davidson, speaking as a charter member of the newly established Balboa Park Protective Association. "Let these funds be used for that purpose, and bring back into their original beauty these world-famous buildings. San Diego is not blessed with too many manmade beauty spots. Let us preserve this one."

In early 1948 that's exactly what the city agreed to do. The buildings would be patched up as much as possible and replaced in permanent materials as available funds (never plentiful) permitted. The initial cost topped $1 million.

Museums reopen

In December 1947 the Fine Arts Gallery reopened. William Templeton Johnson, who designed the original building, developed plans for two wings, but construction was delayed for nearly two decades. In April 1948 the Museum of Man threw open its doors,

continued on page 135

SPANISH VILLAGE AFTER IT WAS ABANDONED BY THE U.S. NAVY AND PRIOR TO RESTORATION, 1947 *San Diego Historical Society*

Spanish Village Art Center, 1957 *San Diego Historical Society*

THE PLAZA DE PANAMA FRONTING THE SAN DIEGO MUSEUM OF ART WAS JUST A PARKING LOT IN CAR-DEPENDENT BALBOA PARK AFTER WORLD WAR II, 1950S. *San Diego Historical Society*

PARK BOULEVARD PASSED CLOSE BY THE NATURAL HISTORY MUSEUM, 1950S, UNTIL THE ROAD WAS RELOCATED IN THE 1970S. *San Diego Historical Society*

THE BALBOA PARK RAILROAD OPENED FOR SERVICE IN 1948, CARRYING UPWARDS OF 100,000 RIDERS SOME YEARS. *San Diego Historical Society*

ORIGINALLY THE NEW MEXICO BUILDING DURING THE 1915 EXPOSITION, THIS BUILDING BECAME THE PALACE OF EDUCATION IN 1935, THE ADMIRAL KIDD OFFICER'S CLUB
DURING WORLD WAR II AND FINALLY THE BALBOA PARK CLUB IN 1948. *San Diego Historical Society*

Model railroad display in Balboa Park, 1956 *San Diego Historical Society*

VIRTUALLY ANY DAY, MEN AND WOMEN ATTIRED IN WHITE CAN BE SEEN ENJOYING LAWN BOWLING AT THE COURSE AT THE WESTERN ENTRANCE TO EL PRADO. THIS VIEW IS FROM 1954. *San Diego Historical Society*

"Learn to Swim Program" at the Kearns Swimming Pool in Morley Field, 1951 *San Diego Historical Society*

followed by the House of Pacific Relations in August and the Photographic Arts Society (in what is today the United Nations Association Building) in November. In January 1949 the House of Hospitality reopened with a concert by the Sinfonietta Orchestra of San Diego. That summer saw the return of the San Diego Symphony, performing for the first time in seven years, this time in Balboa Park Bowl. In November the city's oldest cultural institution, the Society of Natural History, celebrated its 75th anniversary with new exhibits in its reopened museum.

In November 1948 regular service began on the Balboa Park Railroad, but this was a train for toddlers. Gary Peeler, age 3, drove the final spike. Meanwhile, the Conference Building, Palisades Building and Balboa Park Club were offered to folk dancers, craft guilds, puppeteers and numerous other organizations.

As before the war, outsiders always saw ways that unoccupied park land might be put to "productive" use. Park defenders beat back a request by the San Diego Unified School District to build an administrative center in the park. The San Diego Fish and Game Association, sponsors of the San Diego Casting Club, lost its bid to turn the Lily Pond into a fly-casting pool; an interim arrangement was made to allow fly casting at the Morley Field municipal pool during the winter months until a permanent pool in that area could be built.

More successful were highway engineers, who completed the Cabrillo Freeway (U.S. 395/State Route 163) beneath the Cabrillo Bridge in February 1948. In the 1950s they mapped a course for the Cross-Town Freeway, Interstate 5, through the park. The less-palatable alternatives would have run the freeway along Harbor Drive, cutting off downtown from the waterfront, or required eminent domain of even more private property than was already necessary. The taxpayers got a bargain in the ultimate solution, but residents paid the price— noise and air pollution — in the permanent separation between the park and downtown. Ultimately, freeways consumed more than 111 acres of dedicated parkland.

TRAFFIC MOVING ALONG STATE ROUTE 163 UNDER THE CABRILLO BRIDGE, 1957 *San Diego Historical Society*

"Know Your Park"

Once most of the new improvements were in place, *The San Diego Union* ran a series of articles, "Know Your Park," throughout 1950 to reintroduce Balboa Park to the public. One writer naively suggested that still more development would be welcomed: "A huge centrally located expanse of land with varied topography, the park sets no limits on the dreams of those who envision San Diego as a tourist paradise."

One such dream was another world's fair. Clyde M. Vandeburg, a former newspaperman and national expert on expositions, sketched out plans for the 1953 "California World Progress Exposition" in Balboa Park and newly developing Mission Bay Park. "You have the best facilities in the country for the exposition," he said. "And, of course, you have the climate that simplifies operations."

A "Save Balboa Park Committee" sprang up to oppose the fair because it would close the park once again to free public access. The outbreak of the Korean War in June 1950 sidetracked the proposed "showcase for the American free enterprise system and the benefits it has produced." Nearly $200,000 in additional park improvements throughout the city (including $25,000 to rebuild the Botanical Building) were suspended as wartime controls returned. The concept

of holding a big fair in the second half of the 20th century never again took hold. Instead, San Diego made do with festivals, consumer shows and neighborhood street fairs throughout the city aimed primarily at residents, not tourists.

However, new park proposals continued to appear. The minor-league Padres wanted a new ballpark in 1955 to replace Lane Field at the foot of Broadway downtown. The Planning Commission said no. In 1957 voters rejected bonds for a 3,000-seat civic theater on the site desired by the Padres east of the San Diego Zoo parking lot. Convention and Visitors Bureau officials hoped the Ford Building could become a large meeting hall. The experts said in 1959 that was impractical. The only new idea apart from freeway construction to bear fruit: The addition of a children's zoo within the San Diego Zoo in 1957. It was built partly on the site of the 1915 Japanese Tea Pavilion. The central library was housed in the park's Food and Beverages Building (now, Casa del Prado) from 1952 to 1954, while a new library was being built downtown. A park site had previously been rejected by voters.

In 1959 the Botanical Building was the last park structure to be restored. Other Navy-funded restorations did little to secure the exposition buildings' long-term future. Plaster ornamentation occasionally fell from a building, prompting city inspectors to raise

continued on page 140

BOTANICAL GARDENS BUILDING BEING RECONSTRUCTED, 1957 *San Diego Historical Society*

AERIAL VIEW OF A CAPACITY CROWD AT A SAN DIEGO CHARGERS FOOTBALL GAME ON NOVEMBER 26, 1964 — THE CHARGERS PLAYED IN BALBOA STADIUM UNTIL 1967 WHEN SAN DIEGO JACK MURPHY (QUALCOMM) STADIUM OPENED IN MISSION VALLEY. *San Diego Historical Society*

The Beatles at a press conference prior to their concert in Balboa Stadium on August 28, 1965 *San Diego Historical Society*

the red flag of condemnation. "The uses most of the buildings are put to do not justify spending the amount of money required to repair and maintain them," said park and recreation director Leo Calland. "Their deterioration is such they will reach the point where someday they will have to come down."

In May 1957, a 75-member citizens committee, appointed by Mayor Charles C. Dail recommended that some buildings be demolished. Any new structures should be designed "of commensurate beauty" to that of the original fair buildings, the committee said. In addition, the group, headed by Dr. Douglas D. McElfresh, called for better intrapark transportation and parking; no further freeway encroachments; and the eventual removal of nonpark uses as new sites became available. "We were asked to develop the type of park that would best serve the community," McElfresh said, "with no recommendation on economics. Finances are not a part of this study."

A Plan from St. Louis

Those details were left to Harland Bartholomew and Associates of St. Louis, a professional engineering and design firm hired in 1959 to turn the citizen recommendations into a workable plan, estimated at $21.5 million. Bartholomew recommended retaining 13 buildings and demolishing 11 others, some of which were to be replaced with permanent construction. Also envisioned were new roads, relocated parking, more pedestrian spaces, more generous landscaping and better recreational facilities for nearby neighborhoods.

The authors deplored the reduction of the park's 1,400 acres to approximately 1,100 due to school, hospital and freeway incursions, "the great foresight and vision of San Diego's pioneers not being as notable in their successors." But they held out a new vision for the park's role in San Diego's future, clearly anticipating how future residents and visitors might use the park:

"The era of rapid urban growth which apparently is just getting under way is being accompanied by economic conditions bringing about progressive increases in the amount of leisure time. We know that in the San Diego area in the future we will have many more people, probably two million, possibly four million. These people will have much more leisure time; more of them will be older and have specialized recreational requirements; there will be more automobiles and better highways permitting more people to travel greater distances each year, and each year an increasing number of these trips, and from greater distances, will be made to Balboa Park."

As Bartholomew predicted, nonpark events drew the public to Balboa Park. The Chargers began playing at Balboa Stadium in 1961. The Beatles played to a soldout crowd there in 1965. At the same time, the new freeway system made it easy for tourists and residents to get to new attractions, from theme parks to concert venues, from marinas to the mountain cabins. For many San Diegans, Balboa Park was no longer their primary leisure-time destination of choice.

Tempest in a Timken

By the time the City Council took up the Bartholomew Plan in September 1961, Balboa Park's future wasn't the center of debate. The hot issue was the Timken Museum of Art. Architect Frank L. Hope had a designed a modern interpretation of what he called "classic Spanish architecture" in bronze and marble. Council members and the general public preferred replication of the original Home Economy Building, used in recent years as an American Legion hall. "Let us not sacrifice an entire treasure chest for the sake of one gem," pleaded former Councilman Ross Tharp, representing the Balboa Park Protective Association. When Timken lawyer Walter Ames and banker A.J. Sutherland implied that the old masters to be housed in the museum might be moved to another city if their museum design were not accepted, the council relented and approved the building at the same time it adopted the master plan. With 300 people crowded into the council chambers, one speaker, J. Dallas Clark, commented, "I don't believe I've seen a more aroused group of citizens." Two months later, the council approved a new west wing for the Fine Arts Gallery. Architect Robert Mosher defended his modern design as harmonious with the historic style along El Prado. Pat Murphy, a member of the park protective group, dubbed it as "nothing but four walls, a flat roof and a bunch of columns."

There were other mixed signals coming out of the park. Private gifts made possible the 1962 restoration of the Alcazar Garden between the California Quadrangle and House of Charm; the park's first new museum in nearly 40 years, the Aerospace Museum, which opened in February 1963 in the Food and Beverages Building (shifting to the Electric Building two years later); the 1965

continued on page 145

ALCAZAR GARDENS IN FRONT OF THE CALIFORNIA TOWER IN 1957 PRIOR TO ITS 1962 RESTORATION *San Diego Historical Society*

MEMBERS OF THE THURSDAY CLUB INSPECT MODERN PLAYGROUND EQUIPMENT THEY PURCHASED FOR THE PEPPER GROVE PLAYGROUND AREA OFF PARK BOULEVARD, 1967.

San Diego Historical Society

A FAMILY AT A PICNIC POSED FOR THIS PUBLICITY SHOT ON THE LAWN IN FRONT OF THE FINE ARTS GALLERY (RENAMED SAN DIEGO MUSEUM OF ART IN 1978), 1960S. *San Diego Historical Society*

THE FOOD AND BEVERAGES BUILDING SUSTAINED EXTENSIVE DAMAGE AS A RESULT OF AN EARTHQUAKE IN 1968, *San Diego Historical Society*

Timken museum; and, in 1966, the Fine Arts Gallery's west wing and nighttime lighting of the California Tower.

On the other hand, from 1962 to 1988, voters did not match private philanthropy with public dollars. They approved only two park bond measures and rejected seven others. Usually, a majority was in favor, but that was not enough to overcome the two-thirds requirement for passage.

Besides money, policy differences and politics impinged on the park. The City Council at first balked and then relented in 1963 when the United Nations Association lease came up for renewal; the UN was not popular among San Diego's vocal right wing. Strong citizen groups were not popular with the city manager and a City Charter amendment reduced the Park and Recreation Board to mere advisory status. Some new board members advocated an architectural review commission to lord over building designs, but museum directors resisted.

Committee of 100 builds clout

Pressure politics dictated the rise of special-interest groups and Balboa Park received a new source of support in 1967 with the formation of the Committee of 100 (now numbering more than 2,000 members). Founded by Bea Evenson and led by Patricia DeMarce, the group lobbied to replace the tottering Food and Beverages Building with a close replica to be called the Casa del Prado. The park board, led by architect Homer T. Delawie, did not endorse accurate reconstructions of the exposition buildings, but to the Committee of 100, attention to historic detail was a top priority. Voters agreed in 1968 when they passed a bond measure to build the Casa del Prado. "Balboa Park is your most valuable piece of property in San Diego!" the Yes on M committee said. "Don't let it be eaten away!" With some exceptions, the committee's views have held sway at City Hall ever since.

Meanwhile, a most dramatic shift in park transportation patterns took place. A mile's length of Park Boulevard was shifted eastward and traffic was closed off from the Plaza de Panama to the Plaza de Balboa, where a new fountain (named later for Bea Evenson) was dedicated in 1972. For the first time since the 1935-36 exposition days, Laurel Street did not run from Sixth Avenue to Park Boulevard. Motorists would have to detour around the park to get from east to west. Pedestrians now enjoyed a car-free zone, east of the Plaza de Panama. Two additional changes resulted from this shift. The Balboa Park Carousel moved a few hundred yards north in 1968 to Zoo Place, and a building site opposite the Natural History Museum was created for the Reuben H. Fleet Space Theater and Science Center, which opened in 1973.

By the time San Diegans began their year-long 200th anniversary observance in 1969, the park was shining again with new buildings, vibrant institutions and civic pride. A New Year's Day feature in the *Union* by Lew Scarr, "Balboa Park: A Pulsing Heart for San Diego's Culture and Recreation," reviewed the park's history and predicted more changes in the future. "Approximately one-third of the total area is undeveloped today," he said. "Balboa Park is not finished. Neither is San Diego."

Notable changes and additions included the zoo's Skyfari aerial tram in 1969; Centro Cultural de la Raza in 1971; donation of the George Marston family home in 1974 (effective upon his daughter Mary Marston's death in 1987); the East Wing of the San Diego Museum of Art in 1974; and the Cassius Carter Center Stage at the the Old Globe in 1975. Even the Golden Hill section of the park received some attention.

In 1976 Balboa Park's El Prado was placed on the National Park Service's National Register of Historic Places. In 1977, the park itself was elevated to National Landmark status. "Balboa Park is the cultural center of San Diego as well as being a beautifully designed urban area — one of the best planned and landscaped in America," architectural historian Carolyn Pitts wrote in the nomination papers. "The buildings are some of the finest Spanish Baroque revival architecture extant... There are a few remnants remaining of America's expositions — Memorial Hall in Philadelphia (1876), the Museum of Science [and] Industry in Chicago (1893), the empty meadows at Flushing [Long Island, New York]. In San Diego one can see a great deal of the 1915 fair today."

Tax revolt, park stalled

For all these positive signs, the park was not immune from cross-currents blowing throughout the land in the 1970s. Two park measures on the September 1973 ballot failed to muster the necessary two-thirds approval for passage, despite editorial-cartoon support from La Jolla children's book author Theodor "Dr. Seuss" Geisel. Proposition A would have raised $4.5 million for Balboa Park, including funds to remodel the Ford Building for use by the Aerospace Museum.

The mounting taxpayer revolt culminated in the 1978 passage of the Proposition 13 property-tax initiative, which rolled back tax

continued on page 154

PARK PRESERVATIONIST BEA EVENSON INSPECTING CASA DEL PRADO CONSTRUCTION SITE, 1971
San Diego Historical Society

BALBOA PARK CAROUSEL, 1954 *San Diego Historical Society*

PANORAMIC VIEW OF THE BALBOA PARK GOLF COURSE, C. 1966 *San Diego Historical Society*

THIS GATHERING OF TEENAGERS WAS LABELED A "LOVE-IN" BY *The San Diego Union*, 1967. *San Diego Historical Society*

COMPLETED CASA DEL PRADO AT THE TIME OF ITS DEDICATION IN 1971 *San Diego Historical Society*

ANTI-VIETNAM WAR DEMONSTRATION IN THE PARK, 1972 *San Diego Historical Society*

Construction of the Reuben H. Fleet Space Theater, c. 1972 *San Diego Historical Society*

rates and cut into park as well as library, recreational and other programs. Recession and budget cutbacks threatened Balboa Park's financial health. Even the free concerts at the organ pavilion, costing a mere $6,000 annually, faced termination. The San Diego County Federation of Garden Clubs complained that beautiful tiled fountains were deteriorating beyond repair. There were rising worries of crime despite police reports that the park was no more dangerous than any big-city park.

Coincidentally, an equally strong environmental protection movement in the 1970s produced growth management, height limits along the coast and bans on billboards. In Balboa Park, this change of heart saved Florida Canyon from becoming another building site; a master plan prepared in 1976 called for preserving the canyon as an example of the park's natural landscape. But preparing a plan and getting it implemented were two different matters.

The park needed a "czar," wrote *San Diego Magazine* architecture critic James Britton II: "The park superintendent and his design staff have valuable experience on which to draw, but they do not have the authority or even the inclination to ride herd on all the people who contribute parts of the Balboa Park future. So the fact remains that no one is in a position to assure that the whole will be greater than the sum of the parts — i.e., a masterpiece of design. Yet, obviously, the finest park must have the finest guidance. Or sink."

The pro-planning group, Citizens Coordinate for Century 3, which had battled highway engineers who wanted to widen State Route 163, held a two-day "dialogue" in the fall of 1977 to discuss the park's problems and possible solutions. "Created out of the vision of San Diego pioneers, the park has been protected and enhanced by the efforts of innumerable southlanders," conference coordinator Muriel Goldhammer told the attendees at the House of Hospitality. "They have given generously of their creativity, energy and money, and have defended their beliefs in the marketplace of ideas. It is in their spirit that this conference and its backup materials were developed, to provide a forum for today's generation to explore the issues and discuss how the park can serve future generations."

Naval might, fiery sight

The 1970s witnessed the park's biggest controversy in 50 years — the proposal by the Navy to rebuild its hospital in the park rather than to relocate it elsewhere. The uproar resembled the battle of the 1920s when San Diego State proposed to build a new campus in the park. The Navy originally planned to move to Murphy Canyon near Qualcomm Stadium. But political pressure from retired admirals and developers led to the decision to rebuild on the edge of Florida Canyon. No less a leader than Hamilton Marston, George Marston's grandson, argued that the park and hospital could not coexist peacefully for long as each sought self-improvement and expansion. The counter argument by the Greater San Diego Chamber of Commerce held that opposition to the park site could trigger a wholesale reappraisal of the Navy's long-term commitment to San Diego.

In September 1979, 61 percent of city voters approved the Navy's plan, a result short of the necessary 66.7 percent required to remove dedicated parkland from park uses. But the majority

FIRE DESTROYED THE ELECTRIC BUILDING (REBUILT AS THE CASA DE BALBOA), HOME OF THE AEROSPACE MUSEUM, IN 1978.
San Diego Historical Society

THE SHALLOW ROOTS OF THE EUCALYPTUS TREES SOMETIMES CAUSE THE TREES TO TOPPLE OVER IN THE PARK. THIS ONE FELL ON THE CASA DE BALBOA IN 1994.
San Diego Historical Society

vote gave the Navy the political cover to proceed with eminent domain against the city and acquire 36 acres to add to 42 acres to be retained from the old hospital grounds. The $281 million monolithic medical center, opened in 1988, resembled a giant destroyer along Park Boulevard, architecturally and functionally at odds with the park's design and mission. The city got 34.5 acres of the old hospital grounds back in return, but the trade was arguably the worst bargain in park (and city) history. An immense hospital complex now was set firmly, possibly forever, in the center of the park.

Close behind the hospital decision in park disasters was a pair of tragic fires within two weeks of one another in the winter of 1978 that destroyed the Aerospace Museum and Old Globe Theatre. Officials believed they were set by arsonists but the culprits were never found.

The February 22, 1978, fire at the Electric Building was both devastating and ironic. Federal funds had already been committed to relocate the museum to a rehabilitated Ford Building. The Aerospace Museum had sought in vain to move temporarily to B Street Pier, but the San Diego Unified Port District said no. The $4 million in losses included a replica of Charles Lindbergh's San Diego-built Spirit of St. Louis, the museum's most popular exhibit. Numerous other aircraft, memorabilia and documents also were gone. One of the few surviving artifacts was a moon rock encased in plastic.

"This is unbelievably tragic," said Owen Clarke, executive director of the museum. "When you've spent that length of time acquiring history, building something up to where it had international prestige, then see it all disappear in a couple of hours, what else can it be?" A rebuilding campaign started immediately and the museum officially reopened in the Ford Building in June 1980.

The Old Globe took longer to recover. The March 8, 1978, fire razed the 1935 theater and a new facility was not ready for performances for another four years. "There's 40 years of my life there," said Delza Martin, one of the Globe's founding members, the morning after. "It's gone. I don't feel much like talking right now." But the play went on at alternate theaters and on a temporary (now permanent) outdoor "festival stage" constructed in less than 100 days, in time for summer Shakespeare under the stars. After raising $6 million to rebuild the theater, the new Old Globe reopened in 1982. Britain's Queen Elizabeth II visited in February 1983.

The Electric Building's ruins were cleared away and the $8 million Casa de Balboa, a replica of the 1915 Commerce and Industries Building, replaced it in 1982. The San Diego Historical Society moved its archives of books and photographs from the Serra Museum in Presidio Park to the Casa de Balboa's basement. A newly created Museum of San Diego History opened later with the eventual purpose of displaying local history from 1850 to the present. Also new was the Museum of Photographic Arts, the latest in a series of park institutions devoted to the camera and photographers. Third in line was the San Diego Hall of Champions Sports Museum, which relocated from the House of Charm. The San Diego Model Railroad Museum also moved from the House of Charm to the basement of the new building.

The reopening of the Aerospace Museum and Old Globe, completion of the Casa de Balboa and another restoration of the Spreckels Organ Pavilion were bright spots in a recessionary economy plagued by high interest rates and inflation. Many years of deferred maintenance gave the park an image of being shabby. Downtown redevelopment pushed homeless people into the park where they camped behind bushes and in canyons.

The *Evening Tribune* complained of "benign neglect" in a series of hard-hitting editorials in December 1983: "Bums sleep in ravines. Muggers lurk in low brush. The watering system, which keeps this wonderland alive, is old and deteriorated... Financially, Balboa Park is like a proud old mother living on an outdated pension without resources to maintain basic necessities, while her children, seeking their own goals, forget their mother's needs."

Of greatest concern was security. Like many of the nation's urban parks, Balboa Park appeared to be safe in daylight and dangerous at night. Petty thefts, even of potted plants, and car break-ins were on the rise. Violent assaults and a handful of murders shocked the public. Reports of rape, illicit sexual activity in park restrooms, arson fires and uncontrolled bouts of graffiti tarnished San Diego's emerald jewel. Bruce Springsteen later wrote a song, "Balboa Park," that spoke of the park's dark side: "He lay his blanket underneath the freeway, as the evening sky grew dark/Took a whiff of toncho from his coke can and headed for Balboa Park."

Old Globe executive producer Craig Noel found his car broken into one day and the day he received his insurance reimbursement check, his car was hit again. "We have gotten letters from the agents of major actors telling us they can't allow their clients to work here unless we make the parking reasonably safe," Noel told the *Union's* Ed Jahn. More devastating, David Huffman, starring in the Globe's production "Of Mice and Men," was stabbed to death in a park canyon at midday on February 27, 1985. In response, the city instituted a special police patrol and various park institutions hired their own security guards.

A less serious but more intractable problem was parking and access. Blockbuster museum shows, new zoo exhibits and sell-out theatrical performances brought bigger audiences and their cars to the park and the city did nothing to enlarge parking capacity. Exacerbating the problem was the elimination of downtown parking lots to make way for new development, prompting many workers to park their cars for free in Balboa Park. Naval Hospital workers and patients also took up parking spaces in the park. Whenever

officials spoke of charging for parking, there were instant cries of outrage from the public. And yet, the zoo was roundly criticized for chopping down trees to make way for more parking spaces in its lot. In the Plaza de Panama, a few dozen parking spaces remained in what official park policy otherwise dictated should be for pedestrians only. Priorities were clear: cars before people. As the Combined Arts and Education Council wrote the City Council in July 1987, "It is not reasonable to try to recast Balboa Park in the image of 1916. San Diego was not a mobile society then. It is now."

Plans, festivals and revitalization

Traffic, crime, deteriorating park buildings, chronic funding shortages and competing park priorities frustrated the adoption of a new master plan all through the 1980s. Park consultant Ron Pekarek spent several years honing a radical plan that would have shifted recreational and cultural institutions and altered the traffic patterns. But his efforts resulted in stalemate, and a less ambitious plan by Steve Estrada eventually was adopted in 1989. A series of precise plans for separate sections of the park followed.

Unlike the 1961 Bartholomew plan, the Estrada plan had a reasonable chance to be implemented because it did not rely on a fickle electorate to approve construction bond measures. The City Council increased the transient-occupancy tax on hotels and pledged to dedicate a portion to fund revenue bonds that did not require voter approval. The master plan included about $150 million in desired projects on a wish list. "We're going to be able to do this without cutting back on any other municipal services because we have a new revenue source," declared City Manager John Lockwood.

The 20-year master plan and the precise plans — a hefty stack of reports totaling hundreds of pages — outlined in more detail than ever before a new future for the park. They seemed to offer something for everyone.

• Old exposition buildings would be replicated as close to their original design as possible.

• New and expanded museums would be accommodated with minimal loss of park open space.

• Lighting, signage and landscaping would be installed.

• Most importantly, new parking garages and lots would be built and finally allow the Plaza de Panama and Pan-American Plaza to be returned to pedestrian-only zones for the first time in decades.

"We're one step closer to the vision of a park where you can stroll from one end to the other without ever having to compete with an automobile," City Councilman Bob Filner told the *Tribune*.

Over the next few years, the much-debated plans actually began to produce steel-and-stucco results. The San Diego Automotive Museum opened in 1988 in the Conference Building.

The old Naval Hospital Chapel became the Veterans Memorial Center and Museum in 1991. The House of Charm was reconstructed and reopened in 1996; its lead tenant was the Mingei International Museum, a folk art museum that moved from the University Towne Centre shopping mall in La Jolla. The House of Hospitality, also reconstructed, opened in 1997, complete with many of the evocative, Spanish-style decorations restored or reproduced from the building's remodeling for the 1935-36 California Pacific International Exposition.

An enlarged (and renamed) Reuben H. Fleet Science Center opened in 1998. The Balboa Park Activity Center, opened in 1999, provided room for indoor sports and community events next to the old Naval Hospital headquarters building. That same year, the Hall of Champions Sports Museum moved to the rehabilitated Federal Building. The Japanese Friendship Garden completed the second phase of its landscape plan for Gold Gulch Canyon next to the Spreckels Organ Pavilion. Construction began on a $20 million addition of the Natural History Museum. Most ambitious of all was a $100 million-plus proposal in 1999 by the San Diego Zoo to redevelop its parking lot with new exhibits and a giant parking garage.

Other minor improvements — from reconstructed arcades and meticulously tended flower gardens to repolished bronze memorial plaques and colorful directional signs — gave visitors the sense that San Diego was serious about maintaining and improving its central park. Kate Sessions, the horticultural "mother" of Balboa Park, would have approved. Her admirers erected a life-sized statue near Sixth Avenue and Laurel Street, surrounded by flower beds. (Sessions probably would not have approved of that. She did not like statues cluttering up public parks.)

Traffic snarls and parking demands got some attention with the inauguration of a free tram shuttle service from the Inspiration Point parking lot to key park destinations. A new fountain in the middle of the Plaza de Panama gave impetus to the long-planned elimination of parking spaces in the park's central square. But that transformation has to await action in the 21st century.

Crime and security problems were brought under control through the use of police patrols on bicycles and horseback, opening of a storefront police office on El Prado, increased park ranger presence and, most importantly, an improved economy. In a May 1999 survey of 384 residents, only 6 percent mentioned crime as the one thing they disliked most about the park. Asked to name the one thing they liked best, 35 percent replied, "just like being there" or "like the general atmosphere."

Park institutions and department planners became more adept at luring residents and tourists to Balboa Park. Nearly every weekend offered some special event. The museums hosted frequent "blockbuster" exhibitions. Musicians and magicians entertained youngsters. Performances at Starlight Bowl and the Old Globe Theatre drew crowds that extended the festive atmosphere after dark.

Pride of a city

As the new century dawned, Balboa Park was proud again. San Diego's most treasured jewel was polished, popular and primed for greater things. It was the city's official site for celebrating the start of the new millennium.

And yet, challenges and competing pressures remained aplenty. The park's management was buried deep in the city's bureaucracy. Its citizen oversight committees were often left out of the loop when powerful institutions wished to vary from official park plans and policies. Funding was at the mercy of annual budget battles and park supporters faced stiff competition from the city's farflung neighborhoods, whose residents wanted a greater share of park and recreation services.

The park's institutions and organizations numbered thousands of members, but in this multitude was a weakness. San Diegans belonged to the institutions but there was no organization they could join that championed the park as a whole. That oversight may have been remedied by the creation of new bodies, the Balboa Park Endowment Fund and Balboa Park Millennium Society. The fund, operated through the San Diego Foundation, receives donations and bequests and makes grants for park improvements and programs. The society hopes to raise several million dollars in a separate endowment from which to fund parkwide programs in education and outreach.

World's fairs and world wars are not likely in Balboa Park's future. But there are glorious possibilities ahead:

• A bay-park link from Park Boulevard to Harbor Drive, tying Balboa Park back into the rapidly redeveloping downtown San Diego;

• Vibrant new residential communities growing up on all sides of the park as infill housing becomes more acceptable to commuting-averse households; and,

• High-tech-oriented museums catering to San Diego's increasingly educated populace.

As San Diegans ponder the potential in their cherished park, they should heed Samuel Parsons Jr.'s advice of 1905: "To know what not to do and when to stop is about the last thing an artist learns."

This 1,172.86 acres is vast but not limitless. Choices will have to be made in the years ahead as to what belongs in the park and what does not. Who makes those choices and what they decide will determine the fate of Balboa Park in the new millennium.

Japanese Friendship Garden opens. 1991 — House of Hospitality reconstructed. 1999

1990 — Veterans Memorial Center and Museum opens. 1997 — Park hosts Expo 2000.

BALBOA PARK RENAISSANCE FAIR, 1982 *Virginia Forbes Slide Collection, San Diego Historical Society*

Park Map

3 Balboa Park Administration Bldg.
4 Balboa Park Carousel
5 Balboa Park Club
6 Balboa Park Golf Club
7 Balboa Park Miniature Railroad
8 Blind Recreation Center
9 Botanical Building
11 California Tower
12 Casa de Balboa
  A SD Model Railroad Museum
  B Museum of Photographic Arts
  C Museum of San Diego History
  D Balboa Art Conservation Center
13 Casa del Prado
  B San Diego Floral Association
  C San Diego Junior Theatre
  D Casa del Prado Theater
14 Centro Cultural de la Raza
15 Concession Stand
16 Federal Building
  A San Diego Hall of Champions
19 Golden Hill Recreation Center
20 Hall of Nations
21 House of Charm
  A Mingei International Museum
  B San Diego Art Institute
22 House of Hospitality
  A The Prado Restaurant
  B Balboa Park Visitors Center
  C San Diego Police Storefront
23 House of Pacific Relations
    International Houses

24 Marston Estate & Gardens
26 Japanese Friendship Garden
28 Morley Field Sports Complex
29 Municipal Gymnasium
30 American Indian Cultural Center
31 Palisades Building
  A Park Development Administration
  B Recital Hall
  C Marie Hitchcock Puppet Theater
32 Palm Canyon Arboretum
35 Reuben H. Fleet Space Theater
    & Science Center
36 San Diego Aerospace Museum
37 San Diego Automotive Museum
38 San Diego Museum of Art
  A Sculpture Garden Cafe
39 San Diego Museum of Man
40 San Diego Natural History Museum
41 San Diego Zoo Entrance
42 Sandieson Seniors Clubhouse
44 Old Globe Theatre Complex
45 Spanish Village Art Center
46 Spreckels Organ Pavilion
47 Starlight Bowl
48 Timken Museum of Art
49 United Nations Building
50 Veterans Memorial Center
51 War Memorial Building
  A Disabled Services
52 WorldBeat Cultural Center
53 Balboa Park Activity Center
54 Tram Central Station

Upas Street

Group Picnic Area

42

Morley Field Drive

8

Upas Street

Roosevelt Junior High School

Richmond St.

Zoo Dr.

Marston Hills Addition

Boy Scout & Girl Scout Camps

24

Upas St.

OFFICIAL BALBOA PARK MAP 1999 *Stuart White Design*

Balboa Park
Today
Smithsonian of the West

Chapter Four

"*The realm you enter is a living expression of what Southern California longs to be: a subtropical paradise where ideas and vegetation spring from the soil with an incomparable fecundity. To experience it is to be dazzled. And with recent renovation work on landmark buildings, Balboa Park is perhaps in its best shape since the era of San Diego's two great world's fairs.*"

— *Matthew Jaffe*, SUNSET, *1997*

In 1992, *Union-Tribune* staff writer Preston Turegano prepared a roundup on the park, headlined, "Balboa Park: The Smithsonian of the West." The list of museums, playgrounds, botanical wonders and recreational facilities does read like the catalog of the Smithsonian's treasures on the Mall in Washington, D.C. Every few years, Balboa Park advocates speak of luring the Smithsonian westward to a permanent substation in San Diego's emerald jewel.

It had taken decades to get the park in shape and by 1999, at the halfway mark in the 1989 master plan's 20-year lifespan, virtually every corner of Balboa Park showed signs of improvement. Whether it was a new building on the Prado or new benches in the Pepper Grove, a baby panda born at the San Diego Zoo or a headliner at the Old Globe Theatre, the park had never looked better since the expositions. Fears of crime, gripes about grime and grumbles over parking and traffic had diminished.

"Succinctly stated," said a May 1999 study on the public's attitudes toward the park, "San Diego County households are attracted to Balboa Park for several reasons, including its many museums, the zoo, and as a place for relaxing enjoyment and recreation. What park patrons like best about Balboa Park, however, is more intangible. That is, the park's general atmosphere/ambience 'just like being in the park' was mentioned more often than any other single attribute or entity, as the one thing patrons like best about Balboa Park."

A day in the life of the park would start with joggers limbering up at Sixth Avenue and Laurel Street before beginning a run across Cabrillo Bridge and onto the Avenue of Dreams that El Prado was and is. At another corner, nurses arrive at the Naval Hospital. Golfers tee up at the 18-hole course, lawn bowlers arrive in their white shirts and slacks. The streets and paths are washed down at the zoo before the early-bird tourists arrive for a gawk. One by one, the museums open up for a day's adventures by culture buffs. The docents at the Museum of Art are gathering for coffee and an orientation lecture. Meanwhile, grounds crews are revving up their lawnmowers, sharpening their pruning

"Pudgy the Clown" doing face makeups in Plaza de Balboa *Photo by Robert A. Eplett*

Morley Field tennis players *Photo by Robert A. Eplett*

shears and tracking down a broken sprinkler that gushes water down the drain.

What follows is something of a checklist of the park's attractions. The information comes from fact sheets and questionnaires provided by the many park groups in the spring of 1999. No doubt, somebody has been left out or a fact or a date isn't right. But this provides a start to finding the niche you may wish to fill or the interest you'd like to pursue. The attendance figures are for the most recent 12-month period and the address, phone numbers and Internet Web sites are the most currently available.

"San Diego's Park of Dreams" is what *Sunset* magazine called Balboa Park in its June 1997 issue. "City park, open space preserve, architectural treasure and horticultural storehouse," wrote Matthew Jaffe. "The contradictions all work together in Balboa Park, a setting that defines Southern California but is not Southern California, a place central to San Diego that remains apart, where the evanescent has become the enduring."

The park's gardens: Horticultural showplace

Although filled with buildings and admission-only attractions, Balboa Park retains its role as a rest stop for the eyes, whether you're strolling its many pathways or speeding past on Interstate 5.

More than 15,200 trees of nearly 400 species comprise the park's manmade forest. A 1998 tree survey found nearly 5,000 eucalyptus trees, 1,910 palm trees, 1,550 pine trees, 677 oaks, 161 ficus and 59 coral trees.

On the Sixth Avenue side, lined by stately queen palms, are the neatly manicured lawns, cool pines and meandering paths, dating back to the early 1900s when park planners envisioned Balboa Park as an English-style romantic respite from the city.

In the middle of the park is 159-acre Florida Canyon (named for the street that runs through it). Together with Switzer Canyon, it is the park's last remaining large plot still in its relatively naturalistic state. The 1961 Bartholomew Plan recommended its retention "as a living memorial to the efforts of those who improved this same type of indigenous landscape to create the picturesque manmade landscape for which Balboa Park is now best known." Steve Halsey Associates prepared a master plan for the canyon in 1976, but construction of the new Naval Hospital on the canyon's edge in the 1980s and other park priorities have delayed implementation.

continued on page 168

VISITORS AT THE BOTANICAL BUILDING *Photo by Robert A. Eplett*

On the east side of the park are the 250-acre Balboa Golf Course, one of the county's most heavily used; the 50-acre Arizona Landfill; and the 117.5-acre Morley Field recreational center. On the south edge is the 15.2-acre Golden Hill recreation and park area, one of the earliest parts of the park to be improved.

The park's most famous landscaping lies in a series of small, highly cultivated gardens:

Alcazar Garden: Adjacent to the House of Charm, the garden was restored in 1999 to its look during the 1935-36 California Pacific International Exposition. Designed by Richard Requa, the exposition's chief architect, it is planted with 7,000 annuals throughout the year. The garden's Moorish-style fountains and tiles complement the nearby California Tower.

Bird Park: Opened in 1999 at 28th Street at Pershing Drive and Upas Street, this city-block-sized art piece by Robin Brailsford is shaped like a bird and includes drawings and text describing the local bird population. The whimsical landscape is designed to be the children's entrance to Balboa Park. Many adults will start here as well.

Botanical Building and Lily Pond, 1550 El Prado: Built for the 1915-16 Panama-California Exposition and designed by Carleton Winslow, the lathhouse is 250 feet long, 75 feet wide and 60 feet high. Contrary to legend, the building was not the skeleton of a railroad station that was relocated to San Diego from Ogden, Utah. It is filled with 2,100 tropical plants and seasonal flowers, tended by city gardeners. The pond, 193 by 43 feet, is stocked with aquatic plants, such as water lilies and lotus. The lathhouse was restored in 1957 and 1994, the pond in 1999.

California Native Plant Demonstration Garden: Located just west of the Morley Field tennis courts, this collection of 42 drought-tolerant native plants represents a shopping list for backyard gardeners who want to conserve water usage in semi-desert San Diego.

ALCAZAR GARDEN, BETWEEN THE CALIFORNIA QUADRANGLE AND HOUSE OF CHARM, SPORTS SEASONAL PLANTINGS AND BUBBLING FOUNTAINS. *Photo by Robert A. Eplett*

THE DESERT GARDEN ON THE EAST SIDE OF PARK BOULEVARD DRAWS VISITORS FASCINATED BY THIS STRIKING CONTRAST TO BALBOA PARK'S OTHERWISE GRASSY, TREE-FILLED SPACES. *Photo by Robert A. Eplett*

Casa del Rey Moro Garden: Installed in 1935 as part of the redesign of the House of Hospitality Building, the garden by exposition architect Richard Requa was patterned after a Moorish garden he visited in 1928 in Ronda, Spain. When the building was reconstructed in 1997, the garden was restored to its 1935 look.

Desert Garden: This 2.5-acre collection of 1,300 cactus, aloes, euphorbias and agaves on Park Boulevard reminds visitors that San Diego's low rainfall makes this a dry, semi-desert with its own set of plant life. The park's first desert garden was developed behind the Balboa Park Club building in the Palisades area for the 1935-36 exposition. Many of the plants were moved to the present location in 1976. The San Diego Cactus & Succulent Society monitors the health of the Desert Garden.

FDR Grove: Dedicated in 1982 and again in 1999, this living memorial to President Franklin D. Roosevelt honors his support of conservation through the Civilian Conservation Corps in the 1930s and 40s. It is located at Palm Street east of Balboa Drive.

Golden Hill Park: Neighbors in nearby Golden Hill began developing this 15.2-acre recreation area off 25th and A streets in 1889. They constructed a fountain (designed by noted Chicago architect Henry Lord Gay), bandstand, aviary, recreation building, clay tennis courts and golf course; the only remnant of this early work is the fountain, which awaits restoration. Landscaping includes a row of oaks, each commemorating one of the sailors who died in 1905 when the *Bennington* accidentally blew up in San Diego Bay. In 1947 a recreation center was developed with basketball courts, a baseball diamond, children's playground and a new recreation building. After a period of neglect, it has become safer and more attractive along with the rest of Golden Hill.

Japanese Friendship Garden: Opened in 1990, the 11.5-acre "Three Scenery Garden" (San Kei En) of mountains, water and pasture is being developed by a private nonprofit organization west of Gold Gulch Canyon (site of the 1935 gold-rush town built for the second exposition). The entrance is located next to the Spreckels
continued on page 174

MORETON BAY FIG TREE, 1981 *Virginia Forbes Slide Collection, San Diego Historical Society*

BALBOA PARK'S LATEST ROSE GARDEN OPENED ON PARK BOULEVARD IN THE 1970S. *Photo by Robert A. Eplett*

Organ Pavilion. The 561-member garden association drew 34,100 visitors in 1998 before it was closed for the next phase of improvements, completed in September 1999: a pavilion for serving tea, koi pond, strolling-paths and a study center. The garden is a successor to the Japanese Tea Pavilion at the first exposition replaced by the Children's Zoo in the 1957. San Diego's sister-city program with Yokohama prompted development of plans for a new Japanese garden in 1968 and the signing of a 50-year lease in 1984. (Mailing address: 2215 Park Blvd., San Diego CA 92101; phone (619) 232-2721.)

Marston House garden: Kate Sessions, the horticultural "mother" of Balboa Park, selected the first trees for George W. Marston's home in 1906 and architect William Templeton Johnson designed the formal garden in 1928. Now a part of Balboa Park, the house and garden are open to the public and managed by the San Diego Historical Society. (Address: 3525 Seventh Ave.; phone (619) 298-3142.)

Moreton Bay Fig: Perhaps the park's most famous tree is this 64-foot-tall, 12-foot-4-inch-thick specimen planted prior to the 1915 exposition. The canopy spread is 117 feet. Once popular with youngsters for climbing, it has been fenced off to protect it (and them).

Palm Canyon: South of the House of Charm are 450 palms of 58 species within two acres developed in 1912 for the first exposition. A wooden bridge and stairway were added in 1976.

Inez Grant Parker Memorial Rose Garden: Across a footbridge from El Prado on the east side of Park Boulevard, this three-acre garden was funded in 1975 by the Parker Foundation, whose founder had her own rose garden in La Jolla. There are 2,406 roses of 190 varieties that bloom from March to December. City park crews maintain the garden with volunteer support from the San Diego Rose Society. The park's original rose garden, built in 1914, covered about one acre near Sixth Avenue and Laurel Street. It was removed in 1927 and replaced in 1932 by the lawn bowling courts.

San Diego Zoo landscape: Accredited in 1993 as a botanical garden by the American Association of Museums, the zoo is a showplace for plants as well as animals. There are more than 6,000 species of plants, some of which (e.g. bamboo, eucalyptus, acacia, hibiscus) are grown for animal food.

Zoro Garden: Between the Fleet Science Center and Casa de Balboa, this grotto was the site of a nudist colony at the California Pacific International Exposition. Since 1997, park gardeners have transformed it into a butterfly garden by installing plants particularly attractive to butterfly larvae and adults.

San Diego Zoo

Founded: 1916. Membership: 240,000 households and 135,000 children in the "Koala Club." Attendance: 3.5 million. Size: 123 acres.

continued on page 181

POLICE ON HORSEBACK PROVIDE EXTRA SECURITY IN THE PARK. *Photo by Robert A. Eplett*

SIENNA DAVEN-THOMAS, 18 MONTHS OLD, ENJOYS THE SAN DIEGO ZOO POLAR BEAR EXHIBIT WITH HER MOTHER, LAURA BENLOMOND. *Photo by Robert A. Eplett*

BERNOULLI EFFECT HANDS-ON EXHIBIT, REUBEN H. FLEET SCIENCE CENTER *Photo by Robert A. Eplett*

Collection: 4,000 animals, representing 800 species, plus 6,500 varieties of plants. Location and address: Park Boulevard at Zoo Drive, P.O. Box, 120551, San Diego CA 92112-0551; phone (619) 231-1515. Web site: http://www.sandiegozoo.org

For many visitors, the San Diego Zoo is Balboa Park, and San Diego itself, for that matter. The promotional material unabashedly prefaces the zoo's name with "world-famous," in capital letters, and rightly so, for the zoo has led the way internationally in animal exhibition and preservation. Its membership, attendance and budget exceed those of all other park institutions combined. It's Balboa Park's 800-pound gorilla.

Receiving its 123-acre allotment of park land in 1922 and a property tax approved in 1934 that will yield about $4.1 million in fiscal year 2000, the zoo proceeded to build permanent enclosures for its small collection and to welcome new additions from around the world. When the Depression struck, the zoo received federal funds to build a flying cage for birds of prey on Primate or Monkey Mesa, completed in 1937. During World War II, the zoo was one of the few park institutions not taken over by the military. With few other diversions available, admission swelled to 652,500 in the 12 months ending June 30, 1945.

By 1951, postwar attendance surpassed 1 million. The Children's Zoo, moving sidewalks, the Skyfari aerial tramway and heavily landscaped, bioclimatic enclosures have been added over the years to improve the environment for the animals and the experience for visitors. Looking to the future, the Zoological Society's "New Century Zoo" plan proposes to convert its parking lot into more exhibit space (and concentrate parking into one or more proposed garages). Virtually every element of the zoo is being redesigned and rebuilt at an ultimate cost running into the tens of millions of dollars. What doesn't fit in Balboa Park goes to the Zoological Society's 2,200-acre Wild Animal Park near Escondido.

Museums

NOTE: The exhibits and artworks pictured here represent the best of each institution's priceless collection.

Reuben H. Fleet Science Center: IMAX Central

Founded: 1957. Membership: 4,600. Attendance: 650,000. Size: 93,500 square feet. Collection: 80 items in three permanent exhibits. Location and address: 1875 El Prado, (P.O. Box 33303, San Diego CA 92163); phone (619) 238-1233. Web site: http://www.rhfleet.org

A planetarium was proposed as early as 1936 to be built inside the Ford Building (today's Aerospace Museum) following the California Pacific International Exposition. A science museum was discussed from time to time before the city and county of San Diego

American folk art sculpture of a horse, 19th century, at Mingei Museum *Photo by Robert A. Eplett*

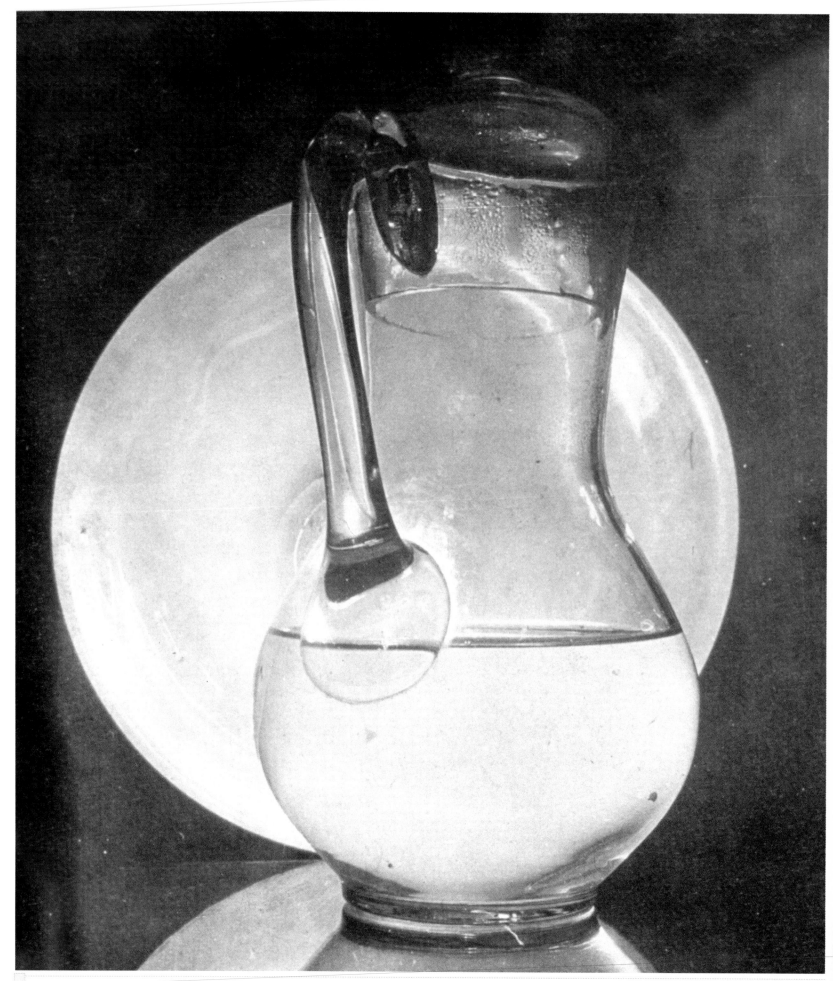

ALEXANDER RODCHENKO'S "GLASS AND LIGHT," 1928 GELATIN SILVER PRINT *Museum of Photographic Arts*

formed a joint-powers authority to build the $4.5 million Reuben H. Fleet Space Theater and Science Center on the present site. It was named for the founder of San Diego's fabled Consolidated Aircraft Corporation (later, General Dynamics/Convair), who donated $400,000. The facility opened in 1973 with an innovative "Omnimax" domed ceiling. The regular program of IMAX films is complemented by scientific exhibits. A major expansion completed in 1998 more than doubled the facility's size.

Mingei International Museum: Folk art worldwide

Founded: 1974. Membership: 2,500. Attendance: 112,000. Size: 41,000 square feet. Collection: 10,000 items. Location: House of Charm, 1439 El Prado (P.O. Box 553, La Jolla CA 92038); phone (619) 239-0003. Web site: http://www.mingei.org

In 1978, San Diego's folk art museum opened in a 6,000-square-foot space at the University Towne Centre shopping center. Its founding director, Martha Longenecker, drew her inspiration from Japanese folk art museums ("Min-gei" is Japanese for "art of the people.") The museum moved into the reconstructed House of Charm on the Plaza de Panama in 1996, The collection includes textiles, toys, handicrafts and art objects representing cultures worldwide.

Museum of Photographic Arts: Stills and moving pictures

Founded: 1972. Membership: 1,500. Attendance: 60,000. Size: 32,000 square feet. Collection: 4,000 works. Location and address: Casa de Balboa, 1649 El Prado, San Diego CA 92101; phone (619) 238-7559. Web site: http://www.mopa.org

Originally operated as the Center for Photographic Arts, a museum without walls, the Museum of Photographic Arts moved into 7,500 square feet in the Casa de Balboa in 1983, sandwiched between the Hall of Champions Sports Museum and San Diego Historical Society's museum. When the Hall of Champions relocated in 1999, MOPA remodeled the space for more galleries, a classroom, auditorium, print-viewing room, library and other facilities. The expansion allowed the museum to develop and screen a collection of motion pictures and videos. The permanent collection includes the earliest forms of photography, such as daguerreotypes and tintypes, and examples of the newest technology, such as laser holograms.

WORLD WAR I AIRCRAFT AT THE SAN DIEGO AEROSPACE MUSEUM *Photo by Robert A. Eplett*

San Diego Aerospace Museum: High-flying feats

Opened: 1961. Membership: 5,000. Attendance: 206,000. Size: 100,000 square feet. Collection: 9,000 items. Location and address: Ford Building, 2001 Pan-American Plaza, San Diego CA 92101; phone: (619) 234-8291. Web site: http://www.aerospacemuseum.org

Honoring San Diego's historic role in the 20th-century development of air and space flight, the museum opened on the Prado with the International Aerospace Hall of Fame. The institution was preparing to relocate to the former Ford Building when, in 1978, arson destroyed its home in the old Electric Building. Efforts began immediately to replace the collection and the museum reopened in the Ford Building in 1980. Among its holdings are a replica of Charles A. Lindbergh's Spirit of St. Louis and a moon rock. The collection is much larger and more complete than before the fire. The museum was the first aero-themed museum to be accredited by the American Association of Museums.

San Diego Art Institute: Local talent

Founded: 1941. Membership: 700. Attendance: 35,000. Size: 10,000 square feet. Location and address: House of Charm, 1439 El Prado, San Diego CA 92101; phone (619) 236-0011. Web site: http://www.sandiego-art.org

Organized in 1941 as the Business Men's Art Club, the group concentrated on learning to paint local historic and landscape scenes. It reorganized as the San Diego Men's Art Institute in 1951, admitted women, adopted its present name and, in 1953 moved to the House of Charm. After the building was reconstructed in 1996, the institute moved back in and continues to showcase the work of local artists.

San Diego Automotive Museum: Car culture

Opened: 1988. Membership: 700. Attendance: 100,550. Size: 30,000 square feet. Collection: 85 vintage cars and motorcycles. Location and address: Conference Building, 2080 Pan-American Plaza, No. 12, San Diego CA 92101; phone (619) 231-2886. Web site: http://www.sdautomuseum.org

This showcase of cars and motorcycles celebrates — and explores — Americans' love affair with the dominant transportation vehicle of the 20th century. The museum displays several dozen classics, many restored by volunteers. Special exhibits explore various themes in auto history. In addition, the research library and resource center offers access to rare publications and a restoration facility gives patrons a glimpse of restoration techniques.

San Diego Hall of Champions Sports Museum: Play time

Founded: 1946. Membership: 550. Size: 68,000 square feet. Collection: 2,500 items. Attendance: 75,000. Location and address: Federal Building, 2131 Pan-American Plaza, San Diego CA 92101; phone (619) 234-2544. Web site: http://www.sandiegosports.org

Bob Breitbard, a former Hoover High School football coach and president of California Linen Supply Company, founded the Breitbard Athletic Foundation in 1946 to honor local high school and college athletes. The foundation opened the first Hall of Champions in 1961 in the House of Charm and moved it into the Casa de Balboa in 1983. The museum reopened in the Federal

1967 MORGAN *Photo by Carina Woolrich; San Diego Automotive Museum*

RECEPTION AT NEW QUARTERS OF SAN DIEGO HALL OF CHAMPIONS IN FORMER FEDERAL BUILDING, 1999 *San Diego Hall of Champions*

Building in 1999 with new high-tech interactive exhibits, a cafe and a gift shop. Among its prized sports memorabilia is San Diego legend Ted Williams' 1941 baseball bat.

San Diego Historical Society and Research Archives: The region's attic

Founded: 1928. Membership: 3,250; Attendance: 51,100. Size: 46,350 square feet. Collection: 17,000 artifacts plus historic photographs, books, art and documents. Location: Casa de Balboa, 1649 El Prado (mailing address: P.O. Box 81825, San Diego CA 92138); phone (619) 232-6203. Web site: http://edweb.sdsu.edu/sdhs/

The San Diego Historical Society made its first home in the Junípero Serra Museum in Presidio Park, built in 1929 by society founder George W. Marston. The research archives were moved to the basement of the Casa de Balboa in 1983 and the museum on the main floor followed soon after. The museum concentrates on 19th and 20th century San Diego history and offers traveling historical exhibitions from other institutions. The research archives contains more than 2 million photographic images of the San Diego region's history; legal, corporate and family records; a library, including oral histories recorded since the 1950s; and architectural drawings and maps. Objects available for display include costumes, artifacts, furniture, ephemera and fine art by local artists. The society also operates the Anna Gunn and George White Marston House museum at 3525

Seventh Ave., designed by William S. Hebbard and Irving Gill and donated by Marston's daughter, Mary Marston, who lived there until her death in 1987.

San Diego Model Railroad Museum: Tireless train buffs

Founded 1980. Membership: 1,200. Attendance: 130,000. Size: 24,000 square feet. Location and address: Casa de Balboa, 1649 El Prado, San Diego CA 92101; phone (619) 696-0199. Web site: http://www.sdmodelrailroadm.com

This display of five model railroads grew out of collections of three clubs: the San Diego Model Railroad Club, chartered in 1938; La Mesa Model Railroad Club, incorporated in 1962; and the San Diego Society of N Scale, incorporated in 1981. The San Diego 3 Railers joined in 1994. The most popular exhibit is a 1/87th scale-model of the San Diego and Arizona Eastern route through the Carriso Gorge north of Jacumba in eastern San Diego County. Balboa Park had a model railroad during the 1935-36 California Pacific International Exposition and in 1949, some of the fair's model builders moved their displays into the House of Charm. They vacated the building in 1978 in the wake of the Old Globe and Electric Building fires and moved into the Casa de Balboa basement in 1981.

San Diego Museum of Art: Old Masters and new

Founded: 1926. Membership: 25,000. Size: 104,100 square feet. Collection: 15,000 works of art. Attendance: 500,000. *continued on page 192*

San Diego Historical Society research archives patrons, Jacque Beck of Ramona, left, and Lucille Griffin of Escondido *Photo by Robert A. Eplett*

The Marston House operated by the San Diego Historical Society *San Diego Historical Society*

THE SAN DIEGO MODEL RAILROAD MUSEUM ATTRACTS YOUNG AND OLD. MICHAEL ALEXANDER AND SON, SAMUEL, 3, OF LOS ANGELES, ADMIRE THE MOUTH OF THE CABRILLO GORGE SECTION OF THE OLD SAN DIEGO AND ARIZONA RAILROAD. *Photo by Robert A. Eplett*

The San Diego Museum of Art, Balboa Park's most well-attended museum, offers the masters as well as examples of popular culture. Robert Page of Mission Valley visits with his daughter Chloe, 3. *Photo by Robert A. Eplett*

"Quince, Cabbage, Melon and Cucumber," c. 1602 by Juan Sanchez Cotan *San Diego Museum of Art*

STELA D FROM THE MAYA
SITE AT QUIRIGUA,
GUATEMALA, AS IT WAS
DISPLAYED AT THE 1915
EXPOSITION.
*San Diego Museum
of Man*

Location: 1450 El Prado (mailing address: P.O. Box 122107, San Diego CA 92112-2107); phone (619) 232-7931. Web site: http://www.sdmart.com

Balboa Park's first art museum was located in the Fine Arts Building, opposite the California Tower, during the Panama-California Exposition. It contained works by local artists and modern masters from the Paris-Luxembourg Gallery. After the fair, local artists continued exhibiting in the building. (Elsewhere in the Fine Arts Building is the Chapel of St. Francis, built for the first fair and still in place as a reminder of the religious overtones inherent in the exposition grounds' architecture.)

In 1922, Appleton and Amelia Bridges offered to build a permanent museum. Mrs. Bridges was the daughter of Henry H. Timken, an Ohio businessman who made a fortune manufacturing roller bearings and other machine parts and retired to San Diego in 1887. The $400,000 Fine Arts Gallery opened February 26, 1926, on the former site of the exposition's Sacramento Valley Building. Designed by San Diego architect William Templeton Johnson, the Fine Arts Gallery was inspired by the 16th century entrance to the University of Salamanca in Spain.

The museum completed its west wing in 1966 and east wing in 1970. The present name was adopted in 1978. The permanent collection includes masterpieces from the Middle Ages to today and the museum has hosted many visiting art exhibitions, from Dr. Seuss drawings to masterpieces by Matisse.

San Diego Museum of Man:
Mummies, baskets and anthropology

Founded: 1915. Membership: 1,600. Attendance: 200,000. Size: 66,000 square feet. Collection: 70,000 items. Location and address: 1350 El Prado, San Diego CA 92101; phone (619) 239-2001. Web site: http://www.museumofman.org

As the first year of the Panama-California Exposition was ending, a group of local leaders formed the San Diego Museum Association to display permanently the exhibits gathered for the fair by scientists from the Smithsonian Institution. Renamed the San Diego Museum of Man in 1942, the institution occupies the entire California Quadrangle plus the adjacent Administration Building. The collection concentrates on native American Southwest anthropology but also includes objects from ancient Egypt and displays on human evolution. The "Plan 2000: The Anthropology Museum for the 21st Century" proposes to establish cultural diversity education and research centers and to host national and international anthropological exhibitions.

San Diego Natural History Museum:
Stuffed birds, gemstones and dinosaurs

Founded 1874. Membership: 5,000. Attendance: 300,000. Size: 150,000 square feet (including new addition). Collection: approximately 7.5 million specimens. Location: Plaza de Balboa, 1788 El Prado (mailing address: P.O. Box 121390, San Diego CA 92112); phone (619) 232-3821. Web site: http://www.sdnhm.org

The San Diego Society of Natural History, the oldest scientific institution in Southern California, opened its first museum downtown in 1912 and moved to Balboa Park in 1917. The Natural History Museum, opened in 1933, was funded largely from a grant by Ellen Browning Scripps. Construction began in 1998 on a north addition. Permanent exhibits focus on the Southern California-Baja California ecosystem and cover zoology, botany, minerals, paleontology, deserts, the shoreline and ocean. Recent traveling exhibits have dealt with sharks, diamonds and dinosaurs.

Timken Museum of Art: Balboa Park's Jewel Box

Founded: 1965. Membership: 218. Attendance: 98,200. Size: 7,500 square feet. Collection: More than 125 works of art. Location and address: Plaza de Panama, 1500 El Prado, San Diego CA 92101; phone (619) 239-5548. Web site: http://gort.ucsd.edu/sj/timken/

Opened in 1965, the museum was the product of two families, the Timkens and Putnams. They reportedly did not socialize with one other but they shared the same attorney, Walter Ames. The Timkens, who built the original Fine Arts Gallery/San Diego Museum of Art, donated most of the funds for this companion museum. It houses the collection of 14th-19th century art collected

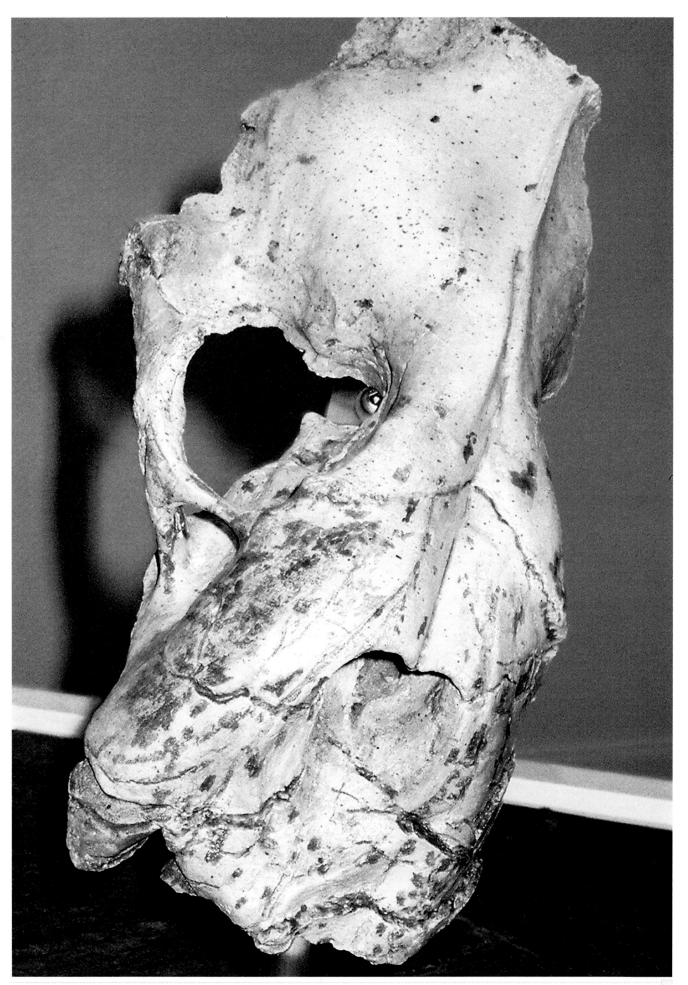

DUSIGNATHUS SEFTONI, SEFTON'S WESTERN-JAWED WALRUS — THE ORIGINAL FOSSIL SKULL WAS RECOVERED FROM 3 MILLION-YEAR-OLD SEDIMENTARY
ROCKS EXPOSED IN CHULA VISTA. *San Diego Natural History Museum*

"Death of the Virgin," Christus Petrus (c. 1410-1472/73) *The Putnam Foundation, Timken Museum of Art*

by two spinster sisters, Anne and Amy Putnam, whose family moved to San Diego in the early 1900s. Ames was president of the Putnam Foundation and his daughter and grandson, Nancy Petersen and John Petersen, carried on his work after his death. Although criticized for not fitting in with the surrounding Spanish Colonial Revival architecture, this modern marble jewel box of art treasures remains one of the few park institutions that charges no admission.

Veterans Memorial Center and Museum: Military services honored

Opened: as a chapel, 1941, as a museum, 1991. Membership: 600. Attendance: 42,000 . Size: 8,000 square feet. Collection: 4,000 items. Location and address: 2115 Park Blvd., San Diego CA 92101; phone (619) 239-2300. Web site: http://www.sdvets.org/mc/veterans_memorial_center.htm

Built as a chapel for the Balboa Naval Hospital, the building was transferred to the city when the new hospital opened in the 1980s. The United Veterans Council, representing 33 veterans groups, leased the building in 1991 and established the Veterans Memorial Center Inc. to operate it as a museum. Exhibits include memorabilia from the Civil War to the present, paintings by local artists and the first American flag to fall in the Philippines during World War II. Transferred to the site was the Vietnam Veterans Peace Memorial, originally located in Old Town.

Other park attractions

Balboa Club: Horseshoes, chess and cards

Founded 1918. Size: 1,043 square feet. Members: 160-200. Location: 2225 Sixth Avenue, San Diego CA 92101; phone (619) 239-7166.

Organized to promote recreation for persons over 50 years of age, the clubhouse was built in 1930 south of Marston Point and rebuilt at the present site in 1961 when Interstate 5 was constructed through the park. Current activities include chess, checkers and card games. The Balboa Park Horseshoe Club also meets at this location.

Balboa Park Activity Center: Net play

Opened 1999. Size: 30,000 square feet. Attendance: projected 500,000. Location and address: Inspiration Point, 2145 Park Blvd., San Diego CA 92101; phone (619) 581-7100.

CHESS PLAYING AT BALBOA CLUB ON SIXTH AVENUE *Photo by Robert A. Eplett*

THE BALBOA PARK CAROUSEL ATTRACTS MORE THAN 100,000 RIDERS ANNUALLY FOR A FOUR-MINUTE SPIN
ABOARD COLORFUL CREATURES. *Photo by Robert A. Eplett*

Replacing space in the 1935 Federal Building, when it became the new home for the Hall of Champions, this facility serves badminton, table tennis and volleyball players and provides an exhibition space for such annual events as the science fair.

Balboa Park Carousel: Round and round

Opened: 1922. Ridership: more than 100,000. Size: 54 figures and chariots. Address: 1889 Zoo Place.

Built in 1910 by Herschell-Spillman of North Tonawanda, New York, shipped to Los Angeles' Luna Park and relocated to Coronado's Tent City, the carousel was moved permanently to Balboa Park in 1922 and to its present location in 1968. For four minutes, riders bob up and down on a handcarved horse, dragon or other colorful creature or grab the brass ring and win a free ride. The original band organ, restored in 1988, plays old-fashioned marches and tunes as recorded on 101 original punched tapes.

Balboa Park Railroad: All Aboard!

Opened 1948. Ridership: 96,600. Size: Half-mile of 15-inch-wide track on 3.8 acres. Location: Zoo Place; phone (619) 239-4748.

The 48- and 36-seat tiny passenger trains were built by the Miniature Railroad Company of Rensselaer, Indiana. The track winds through lush landscaping, past pint-sized Burma-Shave billboards and community signposts. The Zoological Society acquired the railroad and ground lease in 1998.

Casa del Prado: Gardens, plays, musicals and dance

Opened: 1915, reconstructed, 1971. Size: 109,170 square feet. Location and address: 1650 El Prado, San Diego CA 92101.

Built as the Varied Industries and Food Products Building for the 1915 exposition, it became the Food and Beverages Building in 1935 and the temporary home of the Central Library in 1952-54 while the new library on E Street downtown was under construction. Prompted by the Committee of 100, the park support group, voters approved reconstruction bonds in 1968. The building includes rentable meeting rooms for clubs, meeting space for horticultural groups and a 600-seat theater used by dance troupes, the San Diego Junior Theater and the San Diego Youth Symphony.

House of Hospitality: San Diego's living room

Opened: 1915, remodeled, 1935, reconstructed, 1997. Master lessee: House of Hospitality Association. Size: 68,000 square feet. Location and address: Plaza de Panama, 1549 El Prado, San Diego CA 92101; phone (619) 232-2053; Visitors Center, (619) 239-0512. Web site: http://www.balboapark.org

In 1921, an Auditorium Society was formed to manage the exposition's 1915 Foreign Arts Building, which included a large ballroom and auditorium. After it was remodeled for the second exposition, the building received its present name and the society changed its name accordingly. This was the second fair's chief

continued on page 202

BALBOA PARK (MINIATURE) RAILROAD WITH DAVID WEIR AS CONDUCTOR *Photo by Robert A. Eplett*

4419. Foreign Arts Building, corner of Prado and Plaza de Panama, Panama California Exposition, San Diego, Cal. 1915.

THE PATIO OF THE HOUSE OF HOSPITALITY WAS FAITHFULLY RECONSTRUCTED IN 1997 ALONG WITH THE REST OF THE BUILDING AND THE FOUNTAIN AND SCULPTURE, "LA TEHUANA," BY SAN DIEGO ARTIST DONAL HORD. *Photo by Robert A. Eplett*

reception area for dignitaries, including President and Mrs. Franklin D. Roosevelt. After serving as a nurses' dormitory during World War II, the building regained its role as a popular meeting place. A restaurant known as the Cafe del Rey Moro was opened and many weddings occurred in the Del Rey Moro Garden. Following reconstruction, many of the building's former tenants moved back in, including the Balboa Park Visitors Center. A new restaurant, The Prado, opened in the Cafe del Rey Moro's reconstructed space in 1999.

House of Pacific Relations: International cottages

Founded: 1935. Membership: 29 national groups. Location and mailing address: Pan-American Plaza, House of Pacific Relations International Cottages Inc., 2125 Park Blvd., San Diego CA 92101; phone (619) 234-0739.

This 19-building complex was planned by Frank Drugan, the chief promoter and foreign participation director of the California Pacific International Exposition. Exposition architect Richard Requa designed the cottages in his characteristic Mission Revival style with stucco walls and red-tile roofs that were so popular in 1920s and 30s San Diego neighborhoods. During the fair, consular officials occupied the buildings as headquarters and meeting places but there were no exhibits. In December 1936 the House of Pacific Relations was formally opened as a collection of nationality groups

and countries devoted to spread "a note of peace." After wartime duty as Naval officers' quarters, the cottages were reassigned in August 1948 to national groups on a first-come, first-served basis.

Occupying the cottages singly or in pairs are the "houses" of China, the Czech and Slovak republics, Denmark, England, Finland, France and the Philippines, Germany, Hungary, Ireland, Israel, Italy, Japan, Norway, Poland, Scotland, Sweden, Ukraine and Russia, and the United States. The Hall of Nations (the former Press Building) is shared by the houses of Argentina, Colombia, Ecuador, Iran, Lithuania, Panama, Spain and Wales. In 1960 the United Nations Association of San Diego County took over the former Photographic Arts Society/Christian Science Monitor Building adjacent to the cottages and opened a gift shop with souvenirs from around the world. The group currently counts about 400 members and presents six to eight programs annually in the Hall of Nations.

Municipal Gym: From electricity to basketball

Opened 1935. Size: 28,000 square feet. Location: Palisades, 2111 Pan-American Plaza.

Built as the Palace of Electricity and Varied Arts, the design by exposition architect Richard Requa features a combination of Mayan and Art Moderne features. After the fair, it became a gymnasium and reopened for public use in 1947 after the military left.

AT THE CASA DEL PRADO, CAROL POLK OF BURLINGAME (RIGHT), HER DOG HOBBES, AND LYNNE MAYFIELD OF UNIVERSITY HEIGHTS WAIT FOR AUDITIONS AT THE JUNIOR THEATER REHEARSAL HALL TO CONCLUDE. *Photo by Robert A. Eplett*

FIRE ALARM BUILDING AT MARSTON POINT *Photo by Robert A. Eplett*

Old Globe Theatre: The play's the thing

Opened: 1935, rebuilt, 1982. Membership: 9,600. Attendance: 360,000. Size: (1) Old Globe, 580 seats, (2) Cassius Carter Centre Stage, 225 seats, (3) Lowell Davies Festival Theatre, 612 seats. Location: 1400 El Prado (mailing address: P.O. Box 122171, San Diego CA 92112); phone (619) 231-1941. Web site: http://www.oldglobe.org

During the 1935-36 exposition, 50-minute versions of Shakespeare's most popular plays were performed at a replica of London's Old Globe Theatre. In 1937 the newly formed San Diego Community Theatre leased the Globe and began producing plays in the remodeled building. During World War II the theater company performed at various locations and reopened at the Globe in 1947; two years later it began the annual summer Shakespeare Festival. The adjacent Falstaff Tavern restaurant was converted to theater use in 1950 and remodeled and renamed the Cassius Carter Centre Stage in 1969. Cassius Carter was a prominent, early-20th-century lawyer who acted in amateur Shakespeare productions. His son, Armistead, who was active in the Globe, contributed to the new stage's renovation and asked that it be named in his father's honor.

In 1978 when arson destroyed the Globe, productions shifted to a hastily built outdoor stage and downtown theaters until the new Globe opened in 1982. Named the Simon Edison Centre for the Performing Arts in honor of the late husband of a major donor, Helen Edison, it was visited by Britain's Queen Elizabeth II in 1983. The substitute outdoor stage was destroyed by another arson fire in 1984 and rebuilt as the Lowell Davies Festival Stage in 1985. (Davies was a longtime board member.) In the 1990s a new plaza and gift shop were constructed and the Globe leased rehearsal space in the reconstructed House of Charm. The Globe received the American Theater Wing's Tony award for best regional theater in 1984.

Palisades Building: Puppets and recitals

Built: 1935. Size: 20,000 square feet. Location: 2130 Pan-American Plaza.

This was the "Women's Palace" and the "Palace of Entertainment" at the second exposition. After wartime duty, it reopened with a puppet theater (named for the founding puppeteer, Marie Hitchcock), recital hall and craft center. It also contains the Park and Recreation Department's northern division offices.

Spanish Village: Artists colony

Opened: 1935. Size: 6 buildings, 22,725 square feet. Membership: 6 guilds and 31 artists' studios. Location and address: 1770 Village Place, San Diego CA 92101.

Originally, Spanish Village was to be part of a "Villages of the World" complex, including villages representing the Aztecs, Palestine, a Chinese bazaar and other foreign entries at the second exposition. In the end, only the Spanish group was built and it contained shops and restaurants. After the fair, it reopened as the Spanish Village Art Center and included painters, sculptors, jewelers, framemakers and leather workers, plus the Gerde Brothers Marionette Theater and a crafts shop. For three summers, 1937-39, Ralph W. Hastings staged original one-act plays as part of a "Spanish Village Fiesta." After World War II occupation by the 204th Army Anti-Aircraft Artillery Unit, the artists returned in 1947.

Spreckels Organ Pavilion: Popular pipes

Dedicated: 1914; Spreckels Organ Society, founded 1988. Membership: 1,600. Attendance: 100,000. Size: organ, 73 ranks, 4,518 pipes (0.5 inch to 32 feet high); pavilion, 2,400 seats. Location: 2211 E. Pan-American Road (mailing address: House of Hospitality, 1549 El Prado, Suite 10, San Diego CA 92101); phone (619) 702-8138. Web site: http://www.serve.com/sosorgan/

John D. Spreckels, San Diego's early-20th-century tycoon, loved organ music and even had an organ in his Coronado mansion (now, the Glorietta Bay Inn). He originally planned to erect an outdoor organ at his Mission Cliff Gardens at the Park Boulevard terminus of one of his streetcar lines, but then chose Balboa Park's exposition grounds as the site, where his brother Adolph B. Spreckels participated with him in the gift. Los Angeles architect Harrison Albright designed the $66,500 pavilion, built of reinforced concrete, and Austin Organ Company of Hartford, Connecticut, built the $33,000 organ. Dedicated a few hours before midnight, Dec. 31, 1914, opening of the Panama-California Exposition, the organ was a popular attraction at the fair. The Spreckels Company underwrote the organ concerts until 1929, when the city commenced paying the organist's salary. In 1979, the organ and pavilion were restored. The audience area was redesigned for improved handicapped access in 1986.

Starlight (Ford/Balboa Park) Bowl: Musical summers

Built: 1935: Attendance: 40,000. Size: 4,300 seats. Location: 2005 Pan-American Plaza (mailing address: P.O. Box 3519, San Diego CA 92163); phone (619) 544-7800. Web site: http://www.starlighttheatre.org

Ford Bowl hosted symphony concerts and other musical programs during the 1935-36 exposition and San Diego Civic Light Opera (Starlight Musical Theatre) productions from 1948. The San Diego Symphony, which performed at the bowl every summer until 1942, returned in 1949. Both groups moved to other venues in 1967 because of jet noise. Starlight returned in 1975, and the actors and musicians coexisted with the jets by pausing in place whenever a jet passed overhead.

Veterans War Memorial Building: All-purpose meeting hall

Opened: 1950. Size: 21,000 square feet. Location: 3325 Zoo Drive at Park Boulevard. Attendance: 200,000.

Designed by local architect Sam Hamill, the $300,000 building was financed from the sale of the World War II military barracks at Camp Callan on Torrey Pines Mesa. Regular users include eight veterans organizations, 25 dance, senior and recreation groups, and the city's Disabled Services and training programs.

NOTE: Unless otherwise indicated, the following groups and organizations may be reached in care of the Park and Recreation Department, Balboa Park Administration Building, 2125 Park Blvd., San Diego CA 92101, phone (619) 235-1100. Several groups maintain their own Internet Web sites or are listed on other sites. For the most current Web address, use a search engine, such as Alta Vista or Yahoo!

Social and special-interest clubs

Arts and Crafts Council: Founded: about 1972. Coordinates art shows held first full weekend (and sometimes third weekend) of each month on the lawn at Presidents Way.

Balboa Park Program: Started about 1970, this weeklong program sponsored by the San Diego Unified School District introduces about 10,000 fifth graders annually to Balboa Park and its many treasures. Contact: 4100 Normal St., San Diego CA 92103; phone (619) 293-4459.

Blind Community Center: Opened 1949, replaced 1999; 1805 Upas St. Serves about 1,000 of the county's 12,000 blind and visually impaired in a three-story facility; phone (619) 298-5021.

Boy Scouts of America-Desert Pacific Council: 21 acres at 1207 Upas St., San Diego CA 92103; phone, (619) 298-6121. Originally at the first exposition's Indian Village from 1920, the scouts moved to their present site in 1948. Scouts attend weekend and summer camps at Camp Balboa.

Camp Fire Boys and Girls: 3101 Balboa Drive, San Diego CA 92101 (mailing address: P.O. Box 3275, San Diego CA 92163); phone (619) 291-8985. Originally located in a cottage, "Loligro Cabin," on the north side of Morley Field in 1937, the group moved to this 7.5-acre site in 1957. The campsite is called Camp Cahito.

Girl Scouts of America-San Diego-Imperial Counties: 10.5 acres at 1231 Upas St., San Diego CA 92103, phone (619) 298-8391. Originally located in the Pepper Grove on Park Boulevard in 1930, the scouts moved to their present site in 1955.

San Diego Botanical Garden Foundation: Incorporated 1965 to establish a horticultural center in the Casa del Prado; includes San Diego Floral Association and about 40 specialized floral and garden organizations and about 6,000 members. Events include weekly flower shows and meetings every other month.

San Diego Community Christmas Center Committee: Founded 1953 to install holiday season displays every December — a Christmas tree near the Spreckels Organ Pavilion, nativity scenes and gingerbread house in the pavilion and Santa Claus and his reindeer south of El Cid statue; 20 committee members.

San Diego County Carvers Guild: Founded 1993 to introduce San Diegans to wood as art objects and mentor up-and-coming carvers; 26 members meet monthly in the studio at Spanish Village.

San Diego Deaf Senior Citizens Club: Founded about 1976 to provide a social setting for deaf seniors; 45 members meet regularly in the Veterans War Memorial Building.

San Diego Gadabout Senior Citizens Travel Club: Founded 1946 to provide low-cost tours to seniors; 2,000 members meet monthly in the Casa del Prado.

San Diego Mineral and Gem Society: Founded 1934 to promote interest in lapidary techniques and collecting mineral and fossil specimens; 500 members meet second and third Friday monthly (except July and August) in Spanish Village, 1770 Village Place, Building 2; San Diego CA 92101; phone (619) 239-8812. Web address: http://www.san.rr.com/sdmg/

San Diego Trailsetter Travel Club: Founded early-1970s to provide 10-12 low-cost travel trip opportunities monthly for seniors; 2,000 members meet every other month at Casa del Prado.

Southern California Association of Camera Clubs: Founded 1928; includes 16 specialty clubs in San Diego County. Members display their work every Sunday (and Saturdays during the summer) at the Photo Arts Building, 1780 Village Place next to Spanish Village; 11 clubs meet in the Photo Arts Building and five others meet elsewhere.

Musical and performing arts organizations

Centro Cultural de la Raza: 2004 Park Blvd.; phone (619) 235-6135. Founded as Toltecas en Aztlán in 1969; moved in 1971 into former 9,750-square-foot concrete water tank and began offering programs celebrating tribal, Mexican and Chicano arts and culture. The exterior is adorned with murals by many of the same artists who painted the Chicano Park murals under the San Diego-Coronado Bridge. Up to 24,000 people annually attend music and dance programs, art exhibits, classes, lectures and film festivals.

International Dance Association of San Diego County: Founded 1974. The Scandinavian cottages at the House of Pacific Relations hosted folk dancing at the California Pacific International Exposition. The first International Folk Dance Club was formed in 1947, followed by the United Folk Dancers of San Diego, 1955. The group reformed under the present name in 1974 and meets six times yearly to plan events; encompasses 12 clubs that dance once or twice weekly in various park buildings. Web address: http://gb.sandiegoinsider.com/servlets/siteservlet/ida/index.html

San Diego Boys Choir: Founded about 1972 to teach singing to boys aged 7-12; 10-20 members meet Wednesdays during the school year in Casa del Prado.

DISTANT VIEW OF PEPPER GROVE PICNIC GROUND FROM THE JAPANESE FRIENDSHIP GARDEN *Photo by Robert A. Eplett*

San Diego Civic Dance Association: Founded 1945 to introduce children to ballet, jazz, tap and musical theater dancing; adult program added, 1983; 2,600 students attend classes at the Veterans War Memorial Building and perform twice annually at the Casa del Prado.

San Diego Civic Youth Ballet: Founded 1944; 160 students perform in two major productions annually at the Casa del Prado.

San Diego Guild of Puppetry: Founded 1958; grew out of marionette shows given by Marie Hitchcock and her sister Genevieve after World War II. The performances still take place in the 234-seat Puppet Theater (named for Hitchcock in 1988) in the Palisades Building, 2130 Pan-American Plaza; 54 members meet monthly; phone (619) 237-9653. Web address: http://www.puppeteers.org/guilds/sandiego.htm

San Diego Junior Theatre: Founded 1948 to teach acting, singing and dancing to youth aged 4-18; presents five productions annually at the Casa del Prado, Room 208, San Diego CA 92101; phone (619) 239-8355. Web site: http://www.juniortheatre.com

San Diego Men's Chorus: Founded 1985; 90-100 members promote a positive image for gay and lesbian culture; meets every Monday in the Casa del Prado. Web site: http://www.sdmc.org

San Diego Square Dance Association: Founded 1946; 3,000 members belong to 17 active clubs, a callers association, round-dance cuers association, clogging group, contra group and handicap group; roundups held the third Saturday of each month in the Balboa Park Club, 2150 Pan-American Road West. The annual Fiesta de la Cuadrilla is held the first weekend of November. Web site: http://www.ixpres.com/sdsda/

Sun Harbor Chorus: Founded about 1946 to encourage barbershop quartet singing; 11 quartets meet every Tuesday night at the Casa del Prado and perform four Christmas shows annually plus other concerts throughout the year at the Spreckels Organ Pavilion.

Sweet Adelines, San Diego Chapter: Founded 1951 to promote women's barbershop quartet singing; 163 members meet weekly at the Casa del Prado and participate in annual competitions in San Diego and Phoenix.

Twilight in the Park Concerts: Founded 1980; eight members plan free summer concerts at the Spreckels Organ Pavilion.

WorldBeat Center: Opened 1996; WorldBeat Productions, founded 1980 to promote African and African-American arts and culture in a series of education, music, art and dance programs; moved in 1996 to this 12,000-square-foot former water tank; operates radio station KWBC-FM 89.1, offering 24-hour reggae music; shares an amphitheater with the adjacent Centro Cultural de la Raza. Address: at 2100 Park Blvd., San Diego CA 92101; phone (619) 230-1190. Web site: http://www.worldbeatcenter.org

Sports and recreational organizations

Balboa Park Horseshoe Club: Founded 1963 to promote horseshoe pitching: 125 members meet for tournaments monthly at the Balboa Club, 2225 Sixth Avenue.

Club de Pétanque: Founded 1980 to play pétanque, a French form of lawn bowling; about 50 members meet twice monthly at the Pétanqueodome on Morley Field and hold competitions monthly.

Greater San Diego City Tennis Council: Founded 1998 to upgrade 25 existing public courts; affiliated with San Diego District Tennis Association and Youth Tennis San Diego; 40-50 members meet quarterly at Balboa Tennis Club at Morley Field or the Barnes tennis center in Ocean Beach.

Redwood Bridge Club: Founded late 1940s to promote duplicate bridge playing; 200 members meet daily at the clubhouse, 3111 Sixth Avenue, phone (619) 296-4274.

San Diego Archers: Founded 1920s; 50 members practice weekly at the archery range under the Cabrillo Bridge and hold tournaments twice a month.

San Diego Badminton Club: Founded 1930s; 100 members meet twice weekly at the Balboa Park Activity Center.

San Diego Hang Gliding/Paragliding Association: Founded in the 1970s; 120 members meet monthly at the Veterans War Memorial Building.

San Diego Lawn Bowling Club: Founded 1932; 100 members meet daily at the clubhouse and bowling green, 2525 Sixth Avenue.

San Diego Table Tennis Association: Founded 1959; 300 members; games played Monday-Saturday at the Balboa Park Activity Center. Web site: www.sdtta.com

Patrick Sandieson Club: This senior citizen group meets twice weekly in a 1,548-square-foot cottage next to the Pétanquedome east of the swimming pool at Morley Field. The facility includes shuffleboard courts.

BETSY COURT OF THE BALBOA ARTS CONSERVATION CENTER RESTORES THE SAN DIEGO HISTORICAL SOCIETY'S PAINTING BY A.J. ROBERTS WHICH WAS HIS INTERPRETATION OF WHAT THE PANAMA-CALIFORNIA EXPOSITION WOULD LOOK LIKE, 1913. *San Diego Historical Society*

Southern California Velodrome Association: Founded 1998; velodrome built at Morley Field, 1976; 100-160 members meet daily to train for races.

Community advisory groups

Park & Recreation Board: Advises the City Council and city manager. Park and Recreation Department, 202 C St., San Diego CA 92101.

Balboa Park Committee: Advises the Park & Recreation Board, City Council and city manager. Balboa Park Administration, 2125 Park Blvd., San Diego CA 92101.

Community planning groups: Greater Golden Hill Planning Committee, Greater North Park Community Planning Committee and Uptown Planners advise the City Council and city manager on land-use policy in neighborhoods surrounding the park. Department of Planning and Development Review, 202 C St., San Diego CA 92101.

Morley Field Recreation Council: Advises the City Council and city manager on the recreational area in the northeastern corner of the park. Department of Park and Recreation, 202 C St., San Diego CA 92101.

Promotional groups: Christmas on the Prado, Inter-Museum Promotional Council and Passport to Balboa Park Committee oversee special events and administer the discounted multiple-entrance, admission-pass program; 1549 El Prado, San Diego CA 92101.

Other interest groups

Balboa Art Conservation Center, Casa de Balboa, 1649 El Prado, San Diego CA 92101; phone (619) 236-9702. Founded in 1975 by the San Diego Museum of Art and Timken Museum of Art, the nine-member staff restores several hundred art objects annually and conducts conservation and restoration clinics for the public twice each month.

Balboa Park Endowment Fund, c/o San Diego Foundation, P.O. Box 81107, San Diego CA 92138-1107, phone (619) 235-2300: oversees grants for park projects funded from bequests and donations.

Balboa Park Millennium Society, c/o Balboa Park Administration, 2125 Park Blvd., San Diego CA 92101; phone (619) 235-5907. Raises funds to promote parkwide activities and programs.

Central Balboa Park Association: Founded in 1977, this coalition of museums, the San Diego Zoo and other institutions coordinates programs and lobbies governmental officials on matters concerning the cultural center of Balboa Park. Address varies with association chair.

Committee of 100, P.O. Box 19029, San Diego CA 92159: Promotes the preservation of Spanish Colonial Revival architecture in the park; current membership, more than 2,000. Founded in 1967, this group has raised millions of dollars to restore or reconstruct the Spreckels Organ Pavilion and buildings and arcades along El Prado. Web site: http://edweb.sdsu.edu/edweb_folder/sdhs/orderjoin/com100.htm

Governmental and educational institutions

Centre City Continuing Education Center (formerly Snyder Continuation School), 1400 Park Blvd., operated by the San Diego Community College District: 9.9 acres granted by the voters to the school district in 1920.

Naval Medical Center (Balboa Naval Hospital): 78.06 acres granted by voters, 1921-1941, and obtained through eminent domain in 1981 by the federal government.

Roosevelt Junior High School: 17.4 acres granted by voters to the school district in 1920; 3366 Park Blvd., San Diego CA 92103.

San Diego High School and Balboa Stadium: 37.5 acres leased from the city through 2024; 1405 Park Blvd., San Diego CA 92101.

San Diego city: Balboa Park Administration (2125 Park Blvd), park nursery (2850 Pershing Drive), city operations yard (at 20th and B streets), Fire Alarm Building (southern tip of Balboa Drive).

Spanish Village visitors enter from the north side. *Photo by Robert A. Eplett*

Chronology

From pueblo lots to expo palace gardens

1868 City Board of Trustees sets aside 1,400 acres of public lands as "City Park."

1870 State Legislature ratifies the park reservation.

1883 Russ School (San Diego High School) opens on park site.

1887 Howard Bryant's kindergarten and orphanage, Women's Home Association facilities approved.

1889 Golden Hill residents, Ladies Annex improve south and west sections of the park.

1892 Kate Sessions secures 32-acre, 10-year lease for nursery at northwest corner.

1902 Samuel Parsons Jr. hired to prepare park plan; completed, 1905.

1905 City park commission and special park tax approved.

1908 John Nolen proposes "Paseo," landscaped bay-park link, as part of his master plan for San Diego.

1909 Chamber President G. Aubrey Davidson proposes Panama-California Exposition.

1910 "Balboa" chosen as name of park; voters approve $1 million in exposition bonds, $850,000 more in 1913.

1911 Olmsted Brothers resign as exposition planners, Bertram G. Goodhue hired as supervising architect; four-day groundbreaking festival held.

1915 Panama-California Exposition opens; extended into second year as Panama-California International Exposition.

1916 San Diego Zoo, San Diego Museum (of Man) founded.

1917 Navy occupies portion of the park during World War II.

1920 Voters approve 17.35 acres for Naval Hospital (growing to 78 acres later), 17.4 acres for Roosevelt Junior High School, 9.9 acres for continuation school; Boy Scouts occupy exposition's Indian Village (currently, zoo parking lot).

1922 Carousel moves to park from Coronado.

1924 First major restoration undertaken of exposition buildings.

1925 Voters defeat zoo's proposal for autonomy over its portion of the park.

1926 Voters reject 125-acre plan to locate San Diego State Teachers College (San Diego State University) in the park; Fine Arts Gallery (San Diego Museum of Art) opens.

1927 John Nolen prepares new park master plan, proposing what will grow to be the athletic and recreation center at Morley Field.

1930 "El Cid" statue erected in Plaza de Panama.

1933 Natural History Museum opens.

1935 California Pacific International Exposition opens; extended into 1936.

1937 San Diego Community Theater encloses and reopens Old Globe and begins presenting plays.

1941 Navy takes over most of the park at onset of World War II.

1946 Indian Village razed; San Diego Civic Light Opera (Starlight Musical Theater) performs in zoo's Wegeforth Bowl, moving to Ford (Balboa Park, now Starlight) Bowl in 1948.

1947 Museums begin reopening; Frederick Law Olmsted Jr. proposes removing some buildings, restoring others.

1948 Balboa Park (miniature) Railroad begins service.

1949 Old Globe Theatre inaugurates summer Shakespeare Festival; Clyde M. Vandeburg proposes holding the "California World Progress Exposition" in 1953 in the park (an idea abandoned when the Korean War erupted).

1950 Veterans War Memorial Building completed; park improvements suspended at outbreak of Korean War.

1952-54 San Diego Public Library occupies the Food and Beverages Building (Casa del Prado site) during construction of new Central Library.

1957 Citizens committee outlines long-term goals for park.

1961 Harland Bartholomew & Associates of St. Louis submits new master plan; Chargers begin playing at Balboa Stadium; controversy erupts over modern design for planned Timken Museum of Art (opens in 1965); Hall of Champions opens in House of Charm.

1967 Committee of 100 founded to the preserve Spanish-Colonial Revival architecture of the exposition buildings.

1968 Voters approve first major exposition building reconstruction, Casa del Prado (opens in 1971).

1971 Centro Cultural de la Raza moves into water tank on Park Boulevard.

1973 Reuben H. Fleet Space Theater and Science Center opens.

1975 Inez Grant Parker Memorial Rose Garden opens on Park Boulevard.

1976 George W. Marston's home and gardens on edge of park donated by his daughter, Mary Marston, who lives there until her death in 1987.

1978 Arson fires destroy Aerospace Museum, Old Globe Theatre.

1979 Voters fail to grant Navy land for new hospital; property is acquired through eminent domain in 1981 and hospital is completed in 1988.

1980 Revived Aerospace Museum moves into Ford Building.

1982 Rebuilt Globe theater opens.

1983 Casa de Balboa completed on site of Electric Building (former Aerospace Museum home); San Diego Historical Society, Museum of Photographic Arts, Hall of Champions and San Diego Model Railroad move in.

1985 San Diego receives former Naval Hospital property; later moves park staff to two-towered Building 1.

1988 San Diego Automotive Museum opens in former Conference Building.

1989 Soviet Arts Festival features performances, art exhibits in park; Balboa Park Master Plan approved, followed over the next several years by precise plans for various parts of the park.

1990 Japanese Friendship Garden opens.

1991 Veterans Memorial Center and Museum opens in former Naval Hospital chapel.

1995 Tile fountain donated by Mary Elizabeth North completed in Plaza de Panama.

1996 House of Charm reconstructed; Mingei International Museum and San Diego Art Institute are lead tenants; WorldBeat Center of African and African-American arts moves into water tank on Park Boulevard.

1997 House of Hospitality reconstructed.

1998 Zoo proposes expansion of leasehold onto parking lot; Natural History Museum begins north wing.

1999 Balboa Park Activity Building completed at Inspiration Point; Hall of Champions opens in Federal Building; parks hosts Expo 2000, the city's official end-of-the-century, beginning of new millennium celebration.

Overall land use in Balboa Park

Original Total:	**1,400 acres**
Added:	16.54 acres
Subtracted for schools, hospital and roads:	243.68 acres
Current Total:	**1,172.86 acres**
Selected uses include:	
Arizona Landfill:	49.6 acres
Balboa Golf Course:	249.7 acres
Canyons and natural areas:	162.36 acres
City Operations Center:	12.9 acres
Florida Canyon:	124.1 acres
Miscellaneous for museums and institutions:	83 acres
Morley Field:	117.5 acres
Open and play areas:	162.2 acres
San Diego High School lease:	27.6 acres
San Diego Zoo:	123 acres

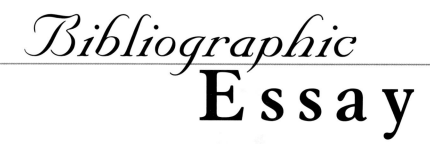

Bibliographic Essay

Despite its long and colorful history, Balboa Park has had only one comprehensive history until this book. *Romance of Balboa Park*, written by the late Florence Christman, published by the San Diego Historical Society and last updated in 1989, contains a wealth of detail about most of the park's buildings.

To enlarge on Christman's work, I turned to an invaluable collection of newspaper clippings and magazine articles copied and organized by longtime Balboa Park researcher Richard Amero. Neatly stored in dozens of three-ring binders at the historical society's archives in the Casa de Balboa, these contemporary news reports are grouped chronologically. Where Amero did not copy an article, he typed the title, date and page number for reference by others. His collection ends in 1992. But researchers can now use the Internet to track down subsequent stories carried in *The San Diego Union-Tribune* and other publications. The chief sources of the clippings were *Los Angeles Times*, *The San Diego Union*, *Evening Tribune*, and *San Diego Sun*.

Amero didn't just copy other publications' articles. He wrote a series of articles himself on many aspects of the park. Some have been published in the *Journal of San Diego History* and others have been posted on his Web site and that of the San Diego Historical Society, as well as included in his collection at the archives.

The *Journal of San Diego History*, published by the historical society, has carried many articles on the park over the years by numerous authors. The work of Gregory Montes was particularly helpful in sorting out the early history of the park. His articles appeared in the Spring 1977, Winter 1979 and Winter 1982 issues.

The historical society's archives contain the best overall collection on park history. In addition to San Diego history books, periodicals, memoirs and its publications, the society owns scrapbooks, photo albums, vertical files of newspaper and magazine clippings and oral histories. The material is more accessible than ever with the advent of an easy-to-use computer database available at the archives.

Primary resources also were consulted for this book. They include the various master plans by Samuel Parsons Jr., John Nolen, Harland Bartholomew, Ron Pekarek and Steve Estrada, plus a variety of city government and citizen advisory committee reports. One happy find was the April 21, 1947, report by Frederick Law Olmsted Jr. After some digging the city clerk's office found the 14-page report to Parks Director W. Allen Perry. A copy went to the historical society's archives for others to consult in the future.

Each exposition had official guidebooks, available at the historical society's archives. Two official park guides following each exposition proved useful in sorting out how the buildings and grounds were used: *Balboa Park Souvenir Guide*, Board of Park Commissioners, 1925; and *A Guide to Balboa Park*, San Diego, California, American Guide Series, Association of Balboa Park Institutions, 1941.

For the history of park organizations and institutions, I relied on questionnaires, press kits, news accounts and interviews. There are only two book-length histories of park institutions — one of the zoo, *It Began With a Roar* by then-*Evening Tribune* columnist Neil Morgan (issued in 1953 and revised in 1990), and the other *Inspired by Nature: The San Diego Natural History Museum After 125 Years* by Iris Engstrand and Anne Bullard, published by the museum in 1999.

Many general histories of San Diego, all available in the California Room of the Central Library downtown or in the San Diego Historical Society archives, deal with Balboa Park. They include:

Richard F. Pourade's seven-volume *History of San Diego* (Union-Tribune Publishing Co., 1960-77) covers Balboa Park in detail in *Glory Years,* 1964; *Gold in the Sun,* 1965; *Rising Tide,* 1967; and *City of the Dream,* 1977.

The Story of New San Diego and Its Founder, Alonzo E. Horton, by Elizabeth C. MacPhail, San Diego Historical Society, 1979

George White Marston: A Family Chronicle, by Mary Gilman Marston, Ward Ritchie Press, 1956

Kate Sessions: Pioneer Horticulturist, by Elizabeth C. MacPhail, San Diego Historical Society, 1976

The Architecture and Grounds of the San Diego Exposition, Paul Elder Co., San Francisco, 1916

San Diego Garden Fair, by Eugen Neuhaus, Paul Elder Co., San Francisco, 1916

Inside Lights on the Building of San Diego's Exposition, 1935, by Richard S. Requa, self-published, 1937

The Magic of Balboa Park, by Andrew Hudson, Photosecrets Publishing, San Diego, 1999

Copies of the original manuscript with footnotes are available from the author and at the San Diego Historical Society and the California Room at the San Diego Public Library. Photographs from the San Diego Historical Society Collection can be purchased at the Society's Research Archives in Balboa Park.

Index

Photo by Robert A. Eplett

Photo by Robert A. Eplett

Photo by Robert A. Eplett

Photo by Robert A. Eplett

Photo by Robert A. Eplett

Photo by Robert A. Eplett

Photo by Robert A. Eplett

Photo by Robert A. Eplett

Photo by Robert A. Eplett